'PATHWAY'

To

BILL + DIANE,

" THANK YOU FOR YOUR
KINDNESS "

HOPE YOU ENJOY THE BOOK

"To know we all are one, - part of the Creator, GOD, the Great White Spirit (or whatever name YOU personally use) is such a wonderful and beautiful thing".

David P Knight   April 1998

'PATHWAY'

THE
CHANNELLED LOVE AND WISDOM
FROM
THE 'TRANSLEATIONS'
THROUGH DAVID KNIGHT

'PATHWAY'

First published in Great Britain in 1998
by DPK Publishing.

ISBN 09532824 06

All the illustrations 'channelled' from the Transleations were computer graphically redesigned by Matt Byron Petch. (Intermedia U.K. Ltd.)

A CIP catalogue record for this book is available from the British Library.

Published by:
D.P.K. Publishing,
The Old School house,
Lowick,
Northants.
NN14 3BH.

Printed and bound in Great Britain by:
Redwood Books,
Kennet Way,
Trowbridge,
Wiltshire.
BA14 8RN.

SEARCH FOR YOUR PATHWAY

I woke so confused in the beginning that was true,
surely there was more to life than feeling so down and so "blue".
I'd ask "Where do I look and what shall I find?"
Then a voice replied, "Just open your heart, your soul and your mind".

So I turned 'within' and found truth, guidance and love,
it came from the Eternal Spirit, the Divine, the Almighty above.
With a light so beautiful, it shone all around,
if you look too, you'll see it's not so hard to be found.

Follow this forever and you will never be lonely, cold or lost,
don't worry, on your 'pathway' you'll discover it doesn't even cost.
Have courage, conviction and in faith please share, it's a plus,
simply take every day, one at a time, there's no need for you to run
or to rush.

On your journey, many people you will meet and good friends they'll
become,
you'll get 'There' I promise so enjoy YOUR PATHWAY, it'll be fun.
Above all be true to yourself and be kind to all and your fellow 'man',
go on, give it a try, deep inside you (and I) know that you can.

ACKNOWLEDGMENTS

To all the 'Transleations', especially to 'Millanderer' and 'Zerrog' and all my guides and teachers on other 'Planes' of existence including; White Cloud, his father White Eagle and Running Bear. You all are so very special and words cannot describe the peace and love you have sent. Without you, this work, this book, would never have been completed. You are in my heart and soul and mind forever.

A SPECIAL 'THANK YOU' TO:

My wife Caroline for all her love, support and encouragement. To Chrissy, Sue, Kevin, Lizzy, Judy, Jen, Jill and my many close family and friends who I have been fortunate to meet and who have helped open my 'Heart and Mind'. To Sheila, for your help in typing this book for me, (bless you always) and to Matt for your superb work on the illustrations. You all mean so much to me and I love you all.

To Tim Moore and June Weller at TWM, to Tony at S&S Print and Lionel at Redwood Books, thank you all for your support to help me fulfil my dream.

THE MYSTERY

(Words that came into my mind on 4.11.94 at 6.55 a.m.)

In my dream herein a beauty lies,
is it clear this meaning or is something disguised?
A race seems on within my mind and I,
try as I might, to unravel these words 'inside'.

In my heart of mine, please, please I yearn so much,
for knowledge, wisdom, truth and guidance and for love.
Forgive me Father if I felt lost and bewildered, but know I've found,
that you're always with me, your 'Light' teaching me and I won't
let you down.

CONTENTS

INTRODUCTION

There are many, many countless questions, mysteries and different pathways ahead of (and for) us all and I hope that there comes a time in your life when the search, the pull of the heart and the longing for wisdom, truth and love fills your very being.

For myself, I was about six or seven years old when, (during a family outing) I gazed from the car window and out over the open countryside, the flashing green trees and rolling hills in the background. "Why am I here?" I asked out aloud. "What am I here to do?" As we continued the family journey I had the strangest feeling that I was here for a reason, but of course not knowing what 'it' was.

At the age of twenty-eight, a meeting with a very special lady called Chrissy (who is a clairvoyant and medium) altered my life. It was from that day forward my life changed in so many ways. Somehow, even the smallest things seemed different including the way that I viewed people, and in how I shared and lived my life.

Wisdom and knowledge and a deep search within and around me became like a thirst, a craving and I needed a direction and understanding of so much more than everyday life. A way opened for me when Chrissy introduced me to Sue and Kevin who took me under their 'wing'. They helped me to become so much more 'aware' and helped open my heart and mind to the Healing abilities (which we all possess) and some psychic 'hidden gifts'.

Over the following three year period I chose to become teetotal and also became a vegetarian and most importantly opened as a being and a soul.

Dreams and dreaming also became a very important part of my life and dream 'teachers' and guides visited and protected me (and still do). After more than two thousand dreams and numerous precognitions*, I knew that my life had changed forever. Meditations and visualisations also played a huge part of what was to come. It was this, together with some 'clairvoyance' received by friends that I knew I had to pick up a pen for these 'channelled dictions'.

During 1994, I telepathically received sentences and poems in my mind. These 'connections' and lines of communication then became even stronger and clearer.

---

* Precognition - Can be simply described as foreseeing a 'future' event. Often received through dream 'state', meditation or indeed by 'other' transfers of consciousness. Many people throughout history have received them including Joan of Arc and Nostrodamus.

Towards the end of the year I had been very fortunate to meet Lizzy, a Crystal Healer. Subsequent healing 'sessions' (utilising the different energy fields of the crystals) enabled me to become a clearer and higher channel for the tremendous love and communication. Then, once my 'Soul Star' and 'Stella Gateway' (transpersonal) Chakras* were in tune, harmonized and open it became even clearer that there was so much more 'out there' and so "PATHWAY" began.

I sincerely hope that this does not sound egotistic in any way. I am nowhere near perfect (and no doubt have many faults) and have a long, long way to go. Learning and living is infinite, it is never ending, but if you can become 'open' and try to live your life to the best of your abilities, then doors will open and 'light and love' will flow in.

If you trust in yourself and love all that is around you then nothing is impossible. Try to be still and be true to yourself to fulfil your destiny. You are all part of each other and are my friends and family of truth and of love and light.

Before you begin to read what has been channelled through me I would like to share the 'teaching' dream received on the night of THURSDAY 25th NOVEMBER 1994. What was revealed in this explained where the 'communication' would be coming from.

Before going to bed I had stood looking out to the night sky and the beautiful stars. It was such a clear night and the stars where shining so brightly they captivated me. I prayed to the 'Great Spirit' and asked, "Spirit, I know of the P's - the Pleiadians** who are communicating with people here, I wondered. . . who, which Entity, Spirit or higher consciousness would communicate with me? I then quickly fell asleep. . .

In the dream I stood at a window looking out onto a horizon. It was night time, but I could see very clearly. Suddenly two large balls of light and a smaller one to the right hand side appeared before me, I suppose like two large 'beacons' (see Picture One: 'BEACONS' page xi). The image then faded.

---

*CHAKRAS: The Chakra system is a *very* important part of our 'bodies'. It could be described as energy points in and around our physical 'self' and is how our spiritual and emotional being enters our physical being.

**The P's, the Pleiadians are the source 'channelled' through a lady called 'Barbara Marciniak'. I have not read either of her books 'Bringers of the Dawn' or 'Earth' which are said to be very enlightening.

Other images then came and faded away too but somehow I knew that they were not linked, I then stood watching the horizon again. A strong feeling of being there (not behind a window) overwhelmed me and I felt movement, just as if I was transported forwards at great speed.

Suddenly they reappeared. They were captivating and so beautiful as they shone like waxing and waning moons. Both were brilliant yellow and white, facing each other. To the right of them I could see a much smaller clearer moon as if in 'orbit'. At this point I heard a sweet and soft voice say "TWO SISTERS" (Picture Two: 'THE TWO SISTERS' page xi).

As the lights/stars shone so brightly at me, my recognition of them was complete for a second only then everything faded and I sadly woke up. (It was 3.45 a.m.) It is hard to describe the tremendous feeling of the scene, the wonder, the beauty and inside of me I knew that something else was to follow.

Over the next six weeks my meditations were very enjoyable but it wasn't until FRIDAY 7th JULY 1995 (10.30 a.m.) that the first long 'communication' arrived. This seemed different though, compared to other 'channelled' works that have been received by people who state that their mind goes 'off' and that they seem to have no physical control over their hand. Indeed, the handwriting produced is very different to their own! (IE. Automatic writing!)

During these experiences I fortunately did not feel this way at all but rather had a 'searching' through and 'in' my mind. As if telepathically* looking for the words to be used for me to write down. I could also stop, start, turn the cassette tape over (I found soft music to be relaxing but not necessary for communication) and also blow my nose and wipe away my tears when emotions and the feeling of so much love overcame me.

A lot of this information came through in verse like poetry, while on other days it came structured with what seemed far more than visualisation and pictures in my mind but more of a realisation!

However it wasn't until the communication of SATURDAY 29th JULY 1995 (1.20 p.m.) that I finally knew that this was a book being 'channelled' and collated. That day and the information received was so beautiful, I will never forget it. (N.B.): These communications would usually last for about an hour, others for an hour and a half or even longer which I found drained me a little, more emotionally than physically. (Although there was always a feeling of the strength and a true connection that seemed around and within me.)

---

* Telepathy: Tele = far off / Pathos = feeling and (or) suffering. (Communication between 'minds' at a distance without the agency of the senses involved. IE. No assistance of the senses or personal memories.)

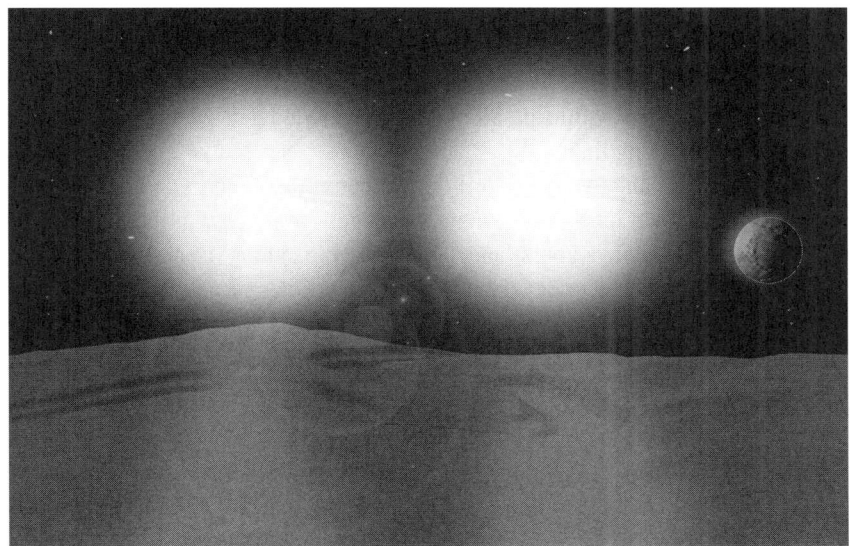

PICTURE ONE: 'BEACONS'

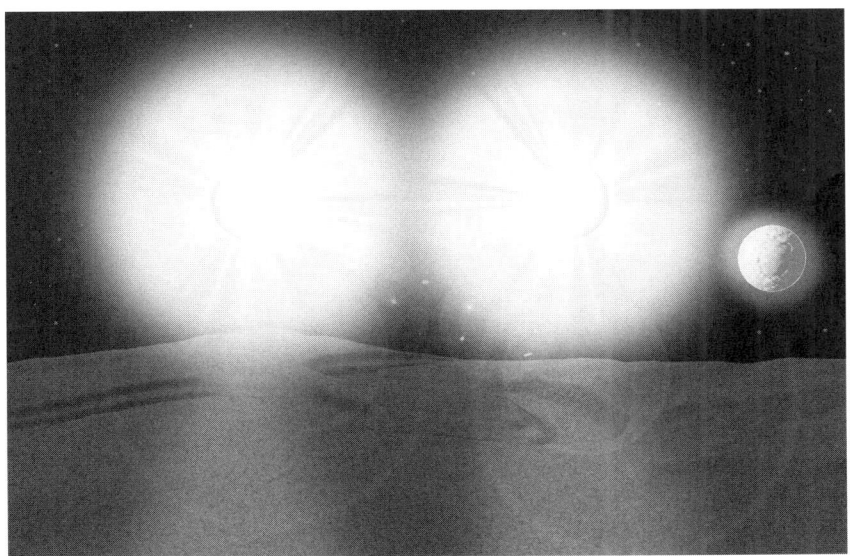

PICTURE TWO: 'THE TWO SISTERS'

Well, enough of me. I really do hope that you can 'relate' to what has been sent and given. Perhaps just one sentence, one page, a poem or even a picture of this book could be the 'something' that can lead you to the peace and love and the light that is within us all. To be acknowledged, needed, shared and deserved by all living things.

No one can change your life or lifestyle but yourself and you are your own judge and your own jury. Your today is also your tomorrow in the making and life's choices are always yours (and should be yours alone) to make.

Finally, I just have to say I have been so privileged and am so proud to have been able to feel and experience all of what has taken place so far. I truly hope that you enjoy this book. Good luck and love to you all.

CHAPTER ONE

'LOVE AND LIFE OR DESTRUCTION?'

FRIDAY 7th JULY 1995 10.30 a.m.

ME: I felt I needed to have a pen and paper to hand. I felt very relaxed and could feel Spirit draw very close to me; a wonderful feeling of peace and love. Thoughts and words came into my head/mind and I began writing. Sentence followed sentence, the words just kept flowing. It was beautiful.

COMMUNICATION: - LOVE. In love we communicate - not to hate or debate. It is not something that is bargained for or used as a weapon, it is sacred beyond imagination.

Love cannot be bought or given for something in return and a sacrifice of love is beyond comprehension. It is everything that man must learn. Once you have learned to love, everything man does becomes easier. Life becomes easier as hate and darkness will be opened up and rays of light will enter in for all to see.

Everyone has their job to do in creating love, peace and truth for it connects everything. Scatter it about and the seeds will grow one by one. Then they'll reach the sky, touching the love that feeds and makes them so high. Every grain of sand and the millions of molecules in your hand contains the love that I speak of, interconnecting with strands of peace and truth, which comes from the great Spirit above.

Listen, please listen to all of your hearts, we are never ever far or apart. So close your eyes and you will see, there is more to life than worry or need. Yes close your eyes and feel this the love and know that the most important gift for you all is from the heart.

Within and above the strength is yours, it is deep inside, forever flowing and ebbing just like your tide. The currents of 'time' only exist in your world, so open your heart to listen and you will find the true 'gold'. It cannot be made, manufactured or spent. It is all. It is everything. It is Heaven sent.

1

So continue to seek and you will find your true 'PATHWAY' to help mankind. Learn to give, not take. For as you sow, so shall you reap the fields of love growing with the Sun. Yes food from above and below. . . it is there for everyone.

Please look and you will know that energy, truth, love and peace is everywhere but every nation and every hand must help in cultivating this true land. Contentment will only be found when the hate and hurt is nowhere around and this will be done, because it will be done by everyone. The seekers of truth grow every day in their different ways and this is, as we have said, okay.

David, I must go now. Time for you to drift and relax, but do not worry my son as I am here, always to return. You are a voice, so let out our truth. Tell all those who will listen that we are sending love abound, for they will find it wait and see. Love always, truth, peace and me. . .

ME: Such emotion poured through me and I feel so fortunate Spirit is in my heart, my soul and my mind. I cannot find the words to tell you how this felt.

I looked through my meditation file and recalled a poem that flowed into my mind back on Friday 3rd February 1995.

Love is a wondrous thing, to be shared by every living thing,
so do not judge each other, be kind to one another.
It is simple this message from the heart,
that we are all one, right from the start.

Our hearts do bleed for you not to kill each other so.
It is not for me to judge you though, so just remember this,
how much love do you give, . . . in a loving kiss?

FRIDAY 14th JULY 1995 11.30 a.m.

ME: Today in my mind I asked about raising my vibrational level* and for wisdom to progress when the time is right. As I sat still I experienced a tremendous feeling of love for me. In my mind an image/sensation of a brilliant gold and yellow light was enveloping and bursting outwards from an open door and doorway. It came to me as if to say 'the door is open'. Then a voice said, 'PATHWAY'. (Picture Three: PATHWAY page 3)

---

*Vibrational Level: This is the resonance of your true 'self' within. We are all at various stages of Spiritual development . . . So your level of vibration would indicate the level that you have reached.

2

PICTURE THREE: PATHWAY

COMMUNICATION: I am here my son and hear you today as always. People always have so many questions but the answers are nearly all the same. This rush, this race, but no one really gains. So be still, and all will come to those who will listen.

Rays of light continue as always to shine through every colour for every creed. Please live in harmony and peace, not greed. There is no greater need other than to live and learn, so do not live with anger or hands on a gun.

The cobweb of confusion mingles with the web of life, but once it is completed only light will shine through so be still, be you, that's all you need to do. Do not try to become someone or something that you are not. People are 'Spirit' and will learn in time through this life, not through crime or in 'what's yours, or mine'. Seek, all of you seek and you will find what is right for you all, but one day at a time. Please slow down, don't rush, as we are here always.

Inside your hearts there is love so strong nothing can erase it, nothing can deceive it. Love so pure you can only imagine the 'light' so strong being sent from 'Heaven'.

The vibrations you speak of David will come in time. They are yours and those of mine, each a different frequency but to become 'one' of a singular consistency so sweet, so harmonious it will ring forever once the door is entered. Push open the door and see the light as it shines for you and mankind forever. Let the Great Spirit guide you all through one by one, like fragments of light of a fallen star he'd left to grow to point in all directions, for *all* to know.

Galaxy upon galaxy will look for this completed light, an example of what is true, of purity, peace and love. 'Beings' that man could not perceive lie in wait to look for this shining 'star' once it's complete. So send your love up and all around for where it ends you'll never know. (PAUSE)

The soldiers of light in every colour from every nation are paving the way for those to follow and create a pathway smooth and wide, marking each door with love and light. Those who see can enter any door and they will find me, as I am Spirit and you are too.

The Great White Spirit does not divide, as I have once explained, between colour and creed so open up and let peace rain in. Wisdom you seek is like a seed. It is small and needs to flourish with the rain and sun to open its shell, letting in the peace so it will grow. In the same way open your heart, your seed, and it will grow with the wisdom, love and knowledge that you seek.

Most people haven't opened their eyes but they will feel the energy and peace it brings and the warmth and love it sends. When you see a clear blue sky, look and feel not stare into open space, for in the sky is everything to see, life, light and the elements that make you and me.

Oh my son, so much you can all learn yet the answers to everything are already there with you.

'Here' the fires of love and light burn so brightly, they are lit eternally so all will see them. As the embers glow, you will all grow and break away forming a new ray of light in your own direction like lines of a compass pointing the way. Like a helping hand across each river and across each land.

The 'light' comes to oversee you all and you eat the light that nourishes your heart, that is why you can never part. It sustains all things as 'White Cloud'* explained. (PAUSE) No I am not 'White Cloud' as you first thought but in the SOUL - a soul. You see a cross in your mind and you are a bit confused, you pause - healing hands is that a clue?. . . I am part of him and you will see, we go hand in hand both you and me.

Things will become clearer but you seem (still) confused, humble is not a word that I would have used. We are all 'one' so there are no high esteems. Spirit does not ever say one is better than another so tell your circle** and all those that you meet, that love and kindness is all you need. . . Now sink, sink into your 'self', you must return to be yourself. Love and light is yours to keep, goodbye my son, peace, truth and me.

ME: Bless you Spirit, for words cannot express how I feel. (Suddenly, after I started to rewrite the transcript more neatly and while playing some music, I felt there was another communication. . .

COMMUNICATION: David, always remember love has no magical number. ONE to ONE makes 'true' (or 2), so let your heart be open. Let it grow and give it a chance to let it know, for inside you is so much. Let it out. . . give to others and be yourself.

It's like a circle and like everything else, give and you will receive. Love hurts and it aches inside so let it free for all to see. Once returned you will never look back.Be strong, be free, in love, truth, peace and me. . .

ME: Thank you 'Spirit' from my heart.

---

*White Cloud - son of White Eagle (the spirit 'guide') who came 'through' with much love and direction in our early development circles.

**Circle - The development circle 'group of friends' formed for meditation and awareness 'get-togethers'.

SATURDAY 22nd JULY 1995

ME: I meditated for a short while before going to work and hoped that some communication would come through. I said, "I just want to say thanks for everything, Spirit!" Straightaway I needed to write down the following words/communication:

COMMUNICATION: 'Once upon a time,' the story goes, where it ends nobody knows. Love and light too sees no final destination, an ending point or finalé. The door is open to all who wish to enter so it is a time for forgiveness and it is a time for endeavour.

Beyond and so far away, lies a resting place beginning to be made of peace and love. No fear or disdain for anything. No pain or waiting to gain - just peace. Oh, if you could see what awaits you all. The splendour, the beauty of love from the 'Divine' linking into everything from 'beings' to mankind. A safe 'house' where nothing evil or bad can exist in minds or bodies - only love and light. (PAUSE)

We shall remain on this frequency for the time being to relate to you what is needed. I hear you think 'we?'. There is more than one of me you see. Keep searching my son and you will find where this is from to help mankind. So far, yet so near for you to think and see and all around is the truth in the air and sea.

Do not be confused because you will know what it is 'to be', but first you must look and continue deep within and then expand your outstretched hand. One step at a time is what is needed right now - we will guide you and you will understand how.

As the night draws in, look into the stars for past the 'Bear' and the Seven Stars lies two small specks, barely seen. This is where we reside to bring peace to thee. The 'Two Sisters' (from these) we are called and not many know this but WE are part of a beginning and many *will* know our name.

Keep your frequency open and we shall be here to teach you what you need to know and we will help pass on the 'Great Spirit's' reasoning and watch them grow.

Our job is a sacrifice to help you all along the way, today, and for as long as is needed. You are part of us and the 'all', just as we are part of you so how can we sit by and not help each other? This is what we should all be doing but only those that will listen will progress to the land of love and light. Guide and be guided and therefore help as many as possible.

You have the need to succeed and you will my son for this web of love has really begun. Look, just look and you will see the two specks you wish to see, burning brightly till our work is done.

We must go now as you have things to do but we will be waiting to communicate with you. Be strong in love and light - be one. Till next time you are with us again, keep strong for love, truth, peace and me.

ME: Thank you from my heart. I will listen and hear you in my heart, soul and mind. Yes, you are part of me and I will work hard to do my best in all we do. Bless you for 'talking' to me so I may help and serve others with your guidance, wisdom, love and protection. This is not 'ego' and never will be - you make me feel so happy and special. I will try to never let you down. Help me to point my pen in the 'WRITE' direction so that my outstretched hand can be seen and your wisdom heard.

YOU are SPECIAL too, and I thank you!

WEDNESDAY 19th JULY 1995: MEDITATION

ME: I felt I needed to meditate today (my day off work). I said, "Spirit. I hope and pray that my guides (and you) can draw close to me this day. I need you so much for your understanding so that I may serve and help others. Please guide me in the affairs of the heart and to help others start their own 'journeys'. Should I write a book with your teachings?" Then, as soon as I started the music. . .

COMMUNICATION: I am here to guide you my son. Do not despair when you are down and think that no one cares; the Spirit world knows and sees all that goes on.

What is in a tear? Happiness, sadness, laughter, despair? All emotions that are deep within to be nurtured along through thick and thin. One day at a time is all to take, no need to lie awake. Look to the light and you will all see the love for you and me but cry when you must because it is a release. 'Heaven' sent these emotions that 'flow', enabling your hearts to grow and grow - these are the things that you all must learn.

Look beyond the surface and all find the true 'you' deep within. Not cold or blue but the warmth and love that you can share which means no more tears of sadness or despair. Search within to find your true 'selves' as this is where true love is. Find your 'self' and you will find love so strong that everything is possible.

7

There are many burning questions in many sad hearts that need direction and that need to part from thinking of oneself. Helping others in a little way will help 'mankind' in a great way. It is the little things that we each do and the things we say that 'light the way'.

As I have said before, the light is strong for you and your friends so go in each of your own directions and you will send the love and the light that is needed to succeed - the 'fourth wave'* yes indeed.

You are the children on the Earth 'plane' right now that carry the torch to light the way for eternity and a day. The Great Spirit has much work for you all to do, to enjoy and realise yourself. You will be fulfiled deep inside, not ego but full of pride. But for now there is much to be done, not much time for play or for fun. . . as the circle of light has more than just begun.

As it spins and moves around touching others from far around, going from town to town, city to city, nation to nation, you will have the strength to wake up the 'creation'. Mysteries will be solved and more answers are what you seek. These are within your grasp and your reach and you will be the teachers to go to the children to teach them the truth and the light. (PAUSE) Please come with me on a short journey. . .

ME: N.B: At this point I seemed to drift off, such space, into 'space' to a planet far away. A hand seemed to come down and let something fall, like sprinkles of light. A tree sprouted up, a tree of 'LIFE'. Stars and comets were whizzing about and then I saw a bird on an ocean wave. Such peace and tranquillity. (Picture four: 'TREE OF LIFE' page 9)

COMMUNICATION: You have the symbols within your heart and the vibrational level to succeed so use it wisely as it is a gift from Spirit to be nurtured and to grow within you. Use your hands in more ways than one and tell those who will listen that love and light vibrations (so strong) will encircle you all.

One by one you will enter the light. Not day, not night but the beautiful light. Brighter than a thousand stars it searches out love and gives to all who see, that includes mankind, you and me.

---

*The fourth wave - deemed to be the 'final' wave of Ascension - Taking the physical 'presence' with the soul to the place where you belong. The first wave has, it is well known, already 'gone'.

PICTURE FOUR: TREE OF LIFE

The door is open so guide all inside and show them your light, your guiding hand. Once they glimpse the beauty inside they will not want to run or to hide. Watch as you now see them crossing over to the wonderful light, brighter than a 'Supernova'. Wave upon wave reaching every corner for all eternity.

Your stars, your Sun, the Earth and Moon may be swallowed up and returned in another way, so make your journey now and you will be saved. Follow your heart, the truth and the light, shine on others and you will be alright.

Moving away to start afresh, a new web of life not a complicated 'mesh'. It will exist on love and love alone, no hate or anger will penetrate this new 'home'. Encased in light for every 'being' to perceive to let them all live and learn. This is the new plane*, your new home. The embers are just beginning but it will soon glow and patiently burn until you, who have made the beauty and the wonder (that you cannot yet imagine) see on your return. Its splendour, its magic, of true life and love with Spirit so close in everything that you will never want for another thing but to live and learn.

In carrying the torch for all 'Worlds' to see, planets so small and so large with millions of moons and 'beings' so uncomprehendable that have been created will be joined for eternity to live as 'one'. The spark has been set and the paper alight, it is down to mankind to live or fight. The World must know that it is not long to go. A few Earth years(?) to make amends and rebuild. To comprehend and to sow.

This is the last chance that will be given for in the sands of time, much has been wasted. Way beyond your natural history lies civilisations who have failed, only 'light' this time will succeed. Understand this my son, day after day find peace and pass it on to those who will listen. Take each day to show them the light so there can be no misgivings. Go in strength those that already see. We are here always. Love, truth, peace and me.

ME: Thank you from my heart Father for drawing so close to me and for your love. You are everything and you are me.

N.B: During this meditation and communication I have never felt such 'vibrations ringing through me'. The heat was unbelievable when the wisdom described the 'frequency' within me. It felt. . . it felt as if something was bestowed - given to me, . . . weird! (I will try to do my best Spirit, to serve and to help others.)

---

*Plane: There are inumerable 'planes' of existence/conscicusness as well as many dimensions of 'time and space'.

SATURDAY 29th JULY 1995 1.20 p.m.: MEDITATION

ME: Guides and teachers please draw close. Help me in my needs so I may serve Spirit and to know myself and to know you. Bless you all.

COMMUNICATION: Welcome again my son. We miss you too. Let things flow like the musical notes and like the wings of a dove.

Energy flows through you all, pulsing from the eternal source of love and light. By connecting and understanding this it will open up many things - wisdom and enlightenment - for when someone realises this, there is nothing that cannot be achieved. Let this flow through is what we ask for you to seek.

Feel the warmth and the capony of love that shines down on you all. As the dawn brings a new sun and the light and warmth radiates over the land, it brings life like a guiding hand just as the growth of a seed or blade of grass grows in the earnest of the light. When the clouds open and the world drinks its life force, it grows. These are the simple things that man seems to have forgotten - what sustains and gives life.

As the tides flow from coast to coast, ebbing and flowing time after time, its movement uncontrolled by mankind because it cannot. . . ever. Mankind must (and needs) to use this principle. It cannot govern nature because it will turn and defend itself. The Earth does not belong to anyone but is free, the air, the birds, the moving sea. There will be a time when you realise this.

We must all live in contentment and peace. This can be done if man really does try. Money too is not important, but to clothe and feed every nation. It means nothing and is only a material gain. All can live together as one if you just give each other a chance. (PAUSE)

A spinning globe will be hit from far, far away; a force so strong that it will be split in two. A light so bright which will be overshadowed in the darkness of the night because the ashes will fall for many, many Earth years and no one will see. Many tears will flow but it may be too late to repair such a beautiful planet created and made for love . . . for will it turn to dust?

There will be a 'moving on' before this happens and those in the light will be safe on the stairway to heaven. A path to another world and a golden gate, the beauty no one can imagine. The wonder, the peace, the love and truth shared by all who enter. The truest stillness ever. . . home.

11

This light will shine one day then the world will see. Any misgivings will be too late to rectify so the damage must start to be cleansed and the dirt washed away which clogs up your hearts. This will take time of course, of which there is little(?) The work has begun and we must all work hard in the time that has been allowed for us. (PAUSE)

David, just relax and enjoy for a moment. . .

ME: I will describe (or try to) what I have just felt and experienced. It was wonderful. I was 'here', then went spiralling upwards through the cloud's which opened up to reveal a circle of light (a Planet?).

Suddenly I am near a waterfall and I am stepping across stones of beautiful colours which light up as I walk, purple, blue, yellow and green. I stand there looking into the water below and I see a key, golden and yellow, shining brightly. A very large dragonfly (?), flies by and somehow picks it up and flies high in the air. I look up in awe at the beauty of everything and as I do, it feels as though the key is dropped to me. . . into me, into myself, through my mouth. Time seems to pass and then I know I am back. (Picture Five: 'THE GOLDEN KEY' below)

PICTURE FIVE: THE GOLDEN KEY

I then continued to receive. . .

COMMUNICATION: The key that you took was a new way, a new door just opening for you. A new 'flow' with which your being is about to start, flourish and open wide the eyes of others. The 'Golden Key' is a sacrifice, point it in the right direction and it will unlock many doors. Many hearts are locked for you to open and the work begun each time.

You make me cry with tears of joy and happiness at your acceptance. Your life has begun in many ways and as your tears flow, ours do too. One day we will be together, our love so strong it cannot weaken. Strands of steel entwined cannot compare. This strength so unique to you and us, always and forever - unique, and never weak.

We are so close now and I know you feel my hand on your shoulder. All is revealed at a steady pace, too much would set your mind and heart a race. Steadiness is called for, for you to develop the right way. Today is another beginning for us to share and where you go we will be there. Your guides and I will always remain so.

Yes love is a wondrous thing my son. So powerful it is the strongest force ever. Unbounding, unrivalled, no distance can break it and a lifetime is nothing for forgiveness' sake. Once each heart is filled with love then our journeys can begin.

Open each heart David with your new key to let light fill and bring in joy that is so bright it will nourish and teach them to grow. Just like the seed, the acorn of love grows in strength and stature, reaching upward to the everlasting light shining down in wonderful splendour. Peace, peace to all your fellow men. So it will be not just for you or me.

The pen will flow and communication too so put everything together in a logical order, collate and demonstrate and spread this around in hardback or paperback. Help will be given to you to do this from there and here and what you feel inside; put it together as best as you can. You will know when the time is right to do this as the help will arrive in different ways.

Choose a cover of golden and yellow (in a picture) that inspires your heart. People will see the picture that you have made and sit in wonder and. . . wonder. You will need a name for calling these works, the name of which you have already written before. A single word is all that is needed to hit the right chord in people's hearts, then the music will flow and the love and light will begin for them. You will be the collator of this work and it must come from within. Simple messages are what are needed, not a racket or din. A song and dance does not need to be made for people to sit up and say. . . "Hey!"

13

There will be chapters 1, 2, 3 and 4 each of varying lengths, 5, 6, 7 and 8 will be the middle to this and 9, 10, 11 and 12 will conclude. People might say the beginning, the middle and the end, but it is only in their mind. There will be this beginning but there will be no end. The 'end' is for them to decide, theirs to create - it is their own destiny that they each make.

Start then with your heart as always and then just let it flow for it will be easier than you think. Someone will help you when you think it is tough, but do not let anyone call your bluff. Page upon page is already set, unlock your key to release your love, our love, Spirit's love, the truth, the peace and me. (Pause). Good-bye, my son. . .

ME: Thank you from my heart, I will do my best and try harder still. I miss you too and you drawing close makes me so happy and I am so proud that I can serve 'Spirit' in whatever is my destiny.

N.B: I feel it is quite apt that I now share with you all a dream received over six months ago on the night of 25th January 1995. I do not want you to think of me as a 'Doomsday merchant' but I can only pass what I receive as I am only the channel or the recipient, and can only say this is what I experienced.

Description from original notes: I went to bed at 10.45 p.m. and it was during the night (Wed. 25.1.95) I'd woken up three times and again at 4.30 a.m. (after three dreams and two multiple 'flashes'*) that I then stayed awake for over an hour. I kept going over and over what I had received in my mind - an immense feeling so strong.... was it to be a long-term precognition?. . . This is what happened.

It is like I am light, in a light and I am watching the bottom of the ocean. . . the sea bed twisting, bursting and cracking open and upwards - severe 'splitting'. . . (A). . . I am zooming backwards and upwards through the sea and the air, an oil rig (?) twists and smashes into the sea, (B). . . then I'm into space. . . the earth cracks and splits completely in two - one half seemed to be sucked in by the 'light' and the other half has the moon dangling from it, (C). Then there is something massive, a huge mass. . . another planet? All touching

---

*'Flashes': My description of 'light' bursting into my mind, usually brilliant white or of a golden yellow/gold. They can sometimes be multiple spectrums or 'bursts' and it is like a door opening to the 'spirit' world and other 'planes' of existence. They are so wonderful and so 'close' that they wake me up.

together with one half with the moon upon it (D). I then woke up with the most weird feeling. It is/was so hard to describe. . . as if there was a daunting task ahead, the end result in question. (Picture six: 'A VISION . . . . . . A COLLISION' pages 16 and 17. This is in four parts A, B, C, D which shows a planet split in two.)

Does some of the communication that you have just read on page 12 link with what I had drawn all those months ago? I will let you decide. One other thought on this, if you have 'love and light' in your hearts then I believe that you will never ever need to worry about this information and vision that is so direct and to the point.

I recalled a poem that I received on 10th March 1995 that seemed to link up with the earlier communication too.

I am both love and light from the great spirit above.
While the earth is dark and the world is grey,
this will be brighter and returned one day.
Go and find and learn, to . . . follow the way,
so that both light and love; you shall seek to save.
Peace and goodwill to all of you;
please open your hearts and minds.
Let the fires of love and light be a source of learning,
that will lead you to the divine.
So go, take good care not to throw away,
your one chance(?). . . to live, we pray.

FRIDAY 4th AUGUST 1995 10.00 a.m.

ME: Please, all my guides, teachers and of course the Great White Spirit, I ask you all to draw close. I need your love, guidance and wisdom for progress - I am here to serve. Reference 'our' book, I pray for more help and guidance and I will piece it together with my heart. (The scene was set and the soft music played). Straightaway. . .

COMMUNICATION: This is a special time for us too and we are glad you have drawn close to us again today, David. Much work for you to do and we will see you through. Peace and love is all around and you have asked for many to draw near and this is so. Do not worry my son.

Okay, let us begin with a story. . .

15

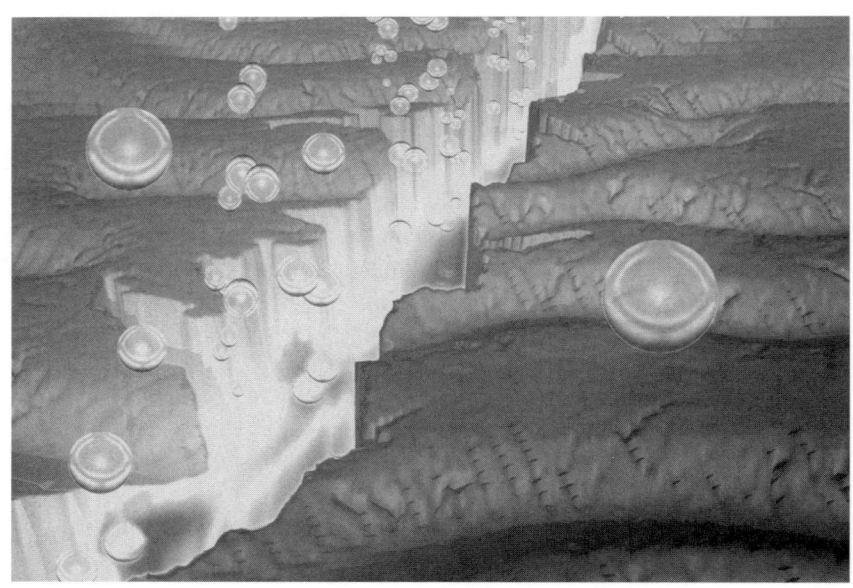

PICTURE SIX A: A VISION . . . A COLLISION

PICTURE SIX B: A VISION . . . A COLLISION

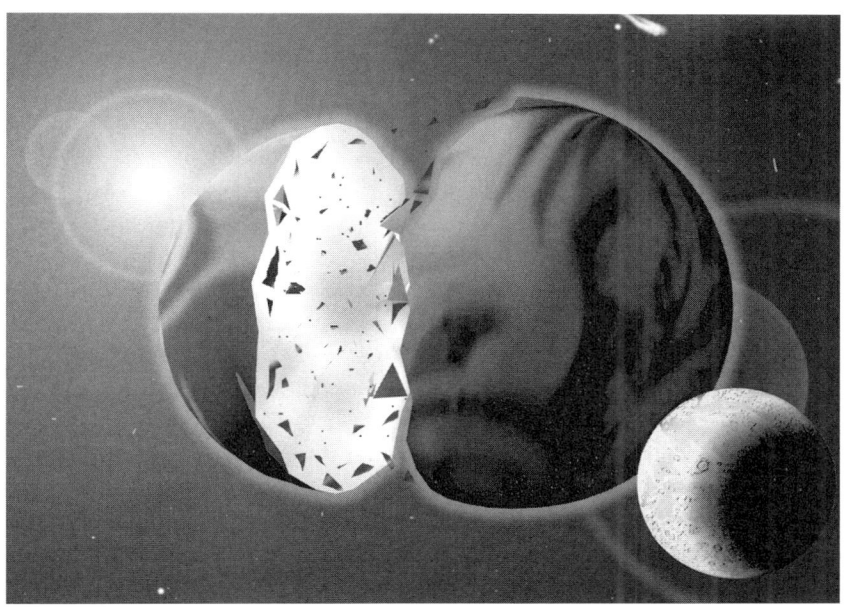

PICTURE SIX C: A VISION . . . A COLLISION

PICTURE SIX C: A VISION . . . A COLLISION

We listen and tell messages from the great Spirit for 'he' has sent messages of love and goodwill which are heaven sent with prayers, rhymes, poems and stories for all to share. Why? Because we love and care.

Draw close all of you who open your hearts and be prepared for we must all learn and listen - a wealth of experience has been too long hidden. Now the book is opened wide for you all to see. May it shine and glisten with instructions and wisdom for you all to share. . . if you care. . . it is up to you.

Once upon a time as a fable starts, this may seem childish but it is a good place to start. A long, long time ago you were all specks of the unknown - no minds to think or say or feel. You have grown so well but have started to diminish your responsibilities to mankind, each other and nature. Cast your minds back, how many trials and tribulations has the world suffered?

I am not going to preach to you but tell you to take stock of your own situation. Expand yourself and look beyond the problems you may have. Look more carefully at the root, the core, the essence of everything and raise your vibrational level and everything becomes clearer - your mind, your soul and everything you say and do.

There is a madness that has grown from seed and is spreading from nation to nation, a destruction of evolution yet many cannot see this. Please, please, please open your hearts and eyes and see goodness for a change and bask in the light. . . the beautiful light.

Many people who have chosen the right 'pathway' have different work to do. Each different, each unique and this is the same for all. Do not judge others because you cannot as it is the divine right of every single one of you to choose what is good and what is right. The destiny you each create is of your own making and wether to live or fight with the gun or knife.

Trace back the origin to when 'time' began, a countless, never-ending span. No beginning and no end. A guiding hand the great Spirit is giving here is a plea from the heart to change your ways and save the day. No pain, no gain is what they say and this is something of what it will take. There is a point in every single one of your lives when you need to stand up and be counted. To make your own sacrifice in the name of love and light but again as I have explained, it is up to you, no one can tell you what to do.

Those in the war zones, the families and children, do you not think that they have had enough? The hurt, the blood and the pain? One day you will all see that it means nothing to move a boundary or state of ownership - my land, your land, whose land? It does not matter whose. Is one man's garden another's deathbed, a killing ground? Rivers of blood and tears will flow in mighty torrents if you do not learn these things.

Those that sit in governments of power playing with others' lives, they are the ones with the extra responsibility for the decisions that are made. They have the cards and the hand to play - they can play a full deck of truth(s) or waste their minds on a 'joker'. Some of them have nothing in their hearts but hate, pain and only want gain. Therefore a lot of change will be down to the 'common' people and 'Mr Average' who can change a lot if he joins his hand with his neighbour.

Link together the hands of love and make a ring across every land. Sow the seeds of love which spiral down like a vortex, a strand of energy for everyone of you. Though there may be a time when many will say, "put this off to another day, we will be alright, we will be okay - someone else's job, someone else's day". These blind decisions will have a catastrophic effect because it 'signals' about and ill thoughts seem to flourish at great speed sometimes, which is hard to comprehend.

We ask, 'why the greed and want of material gain and the 'I' and to get the upper hand?' What is yours or what is mine, is and has much more to do than talk. You fight and squabble about unimportant things. Just turn to the light and love coming from all around you and above. Open yourselves, it must come from you. When you trust it becomes much easier for us to help you so wait and see, there is much in store for you and me. Pause for a moment and just. . . let be. . .

ME: My consciousness seemed to expand and it was wonderful. At first I seemed to be in a cave, a beam of light taking me up and up, spiralling. I could see cliffs, England, up and up, clouds, sky then space. The Earth being sprinkled with 'light' *and a feeling of* overwhelming peace and love surrounded it. I seemed to be like a bird, a beautiful white bird flying through the air before coming back into 'myself'. . .(Picture Seven: 'UP AND BEYOND, ALONE BUT TOGETHER' Page 20)

At this point I then saw something between the 'clouds', but I am afraid that I am not privileged to share it with you. Suffice to say that it was in connection with the strongest and clearest vision/precognition I have experienced just a few nights ago. (It would be unfair to the people and their families and all concerned with them). I appreciate also, that whatever *your* beliefs are in death - I believe it is a rebirth. So all I can say is, "Don't worry - death is 'life' to be continued." NB: Much is to be learned later in this book on this.

PICTURE SEVEN: UP AND BEYOND,   ALONE BUT TOGETHER

COMMUNICATION: Contd. . . Water flows like love down a stream, smoothing and rolling the pebbles and stones back to its origin and one by one seeking its home, its shore, where it needs to roll no more. The rays of the sun warm the water, increasing its temperature and molecular structure.

The rays of love do just the same, so listen to the voice of the master and the teacher. Begin the journey and roll slowly at first, gathering pace and quenching your thirst. Drink the rays of love and strengthen yourselves, gathering speed and embracing each 'self'.

As the swirling sea pushes you from side to side it moves your love from the inside and out. The faster you go and stronger too, means you 'out loud can shout'.

The colours of the spectrum joining as one, in brilliant wonder from the loving sun. Joining with others to hear the truth from the source, the knowledge and wisdom from the only true one. The journey started at full pace now nearing the shore not a second before. A time slot for the pebble, the stone, the other you - revealing the softer more gentler you.

Home now and your safe and sound and a new life begun, a wondrous thing when you are reborn my son. A welcome from family, friends and all those you have ever known, this time holding you close and you won't have to go. Peace, tranquillity and love for those I say, who have completed their journey and their short stay.

If you have done the work and a job well done, you will feel the love forever from the golden true one. A mass of energy not to comprehend, giving out love that never ends. It seeks and it finds and nurtures everything from the beginning to the. . . beginning - no end.

The circle of life goes on for an eternity, will you all join us? Is that a certainty? Those that follow the truth and the light must try to save and seek as hard as you might, show your hand and whisper words of truth, not fight. Yes love for all and every living thing, from the smallest ant to the tallest tree. To kill them all you destroy yourselves, the truth and me.

Time is drawing near again my son, love as always and. . .

ME: At this point I felt the immense closeness of 'Spirit' and of love that I broke down. . . so strange are these tears of sadness, yet also of such joy.

COMMUNICATION: Oh, David, we miss you so. We are watching you grow and grow. Be still, be true and above all be one. We are close. We are near you always and the work will be done, good-bye and. . .

ME: No! Please, please don't go. I. . . (here I could sense and feel such love and strength of 'Spirit' close to me).

COMMUNICATION: The tears that flow contain true gold, David. You fill our hearts and we miss you so. Peace, calm down, be still. A ray of golden light falls upon you and my hand is on your shoulder. You are truth and you will succeed, never fear or doubt or let your heart bleed. We are watching every day and every night to keep you safe and in the light.

Till we meet again and the frequency connects, be still, be you, be strong. My friend, my son, you are close to me. Be strong and the time will pass until you are home again. Love from all of us. Goodbye, peace, truth and me.

ME: I don't think words could describe how I felt. (I wonder how you would feel?)

I read the communication afterwards and such feelings still filled my very being. Something rang like a bell within me and I looked through my journal to find a poem that 'came through' as a communication in a short meditation on the 9th June 1995. It seems to belong right here. . .

So much feeling of love all around, keeping me safe and oh so sound,
a healing inside working away, each and every night and day.
Love, light, peace and tranquillity; what will your gift and ability be,
it doesn't matter what you do, as long as you do your best and be true.

Do not cry and fall down my friend, we are here and will lend a hand,
of golden light and rays that mend, to a broken heart, a well of love we'll send.
A journey begins on a never ending road, a beaten track or a dusty lane,
are these Pathways that you'll follow in vain?
Remember, it doesn't matter what you do, we are always, forever, part of you.

Not a trial, written test or to be the best,
but all is in trying to be and become.
What is in your heart, very being and your soul,
inside and out a glow of love, Heaven sent to you all.

WEDNESDAY 9th AUGUST 1995 10.00 a.m.

ME: Great Spirit please draw close. Please forgive me in my misgivings. I need to learn and need your strength sometimes too. Help me to learn to help myself and to give help to others.

Sorry if I have let you down. Please nurture me, I need to grow with you - always one, always together through thick and thin. I love you all. Please draw close. (Then straightaway. . .)

COMMUNICATION: David! Welcome again my son. We know of the things that you have gone through and the 'tests' that you came through and all the things that you do not understand. It is okay that you feel the way you do, you are not perfect, who is? Just do your best and you will pass the overall test.

Be patient my son. One step at a time as we have already explained, this is your time to gain. Your strength is okay, it is with ours - understand this my son. So good to be together again in peace and love always to be strong. Let us begin our work together. . .

We ask, who is the true man? The blind beggar or the rich man? No one you see, is above or below each other. Who can really 'see', he who thinks or he who can see? Is it you, or is it me or thee? So many people have closed their eyes to their true selves and what they can become. Turn back the pages of history and you will see many 'Bums' (your terms, not ours) who have become 'one'. There is never too late a time to change someone's ways, never too late to fill your days with a challenge for each and everyone. (PAUSE)

Each living speck of consciousness and all life can turn their head to the Sun, the great Spirit's wonderful creation giving out light and love. Feel the energy and vibrations it sends, giving and sustaining life on yours and other worlds. This is but only one sun he has created. There are many. Some smaller and some so many times bigger than in your galaxy each sustaining and giving life, light and warmth.

You must all look beyond your own boundaries that you yourselves have created. Everything is all and all is everything. Know that at the end of the day no one really owns anything. It is all in your minds but you are one of a kind and we understand this. Look beyond 'self' and material gain and you can all grow away from any pain. Give not take and learn to live as one and you can all then, 'become'.

23

As I said before, there is a time when you will all reflect and know what it is you are here for. The seed will grow and will flower into the beautiful light shining so proud, it will light up your night. No darkness or pain where you will go, somewhere you can only grow.

First the work is to be done and the needs of many, to give or to spend a single penny? Harping on is not what we wish to do but 'gimme, gimme, gimme, take, take, take, mine, mine, mine' equals so much greed and so much hate. Where is everybody's love to donate?

We can see the daily turmoil in everyone's lives in what they battle and strive to achieve. Yes we all have responsibilities for the family, the children and our pets, but imagine you are casting out a huge net. If you have love within your hearts you can cast it out so far and wide, not just in and around your immediate next of kin but everywhere you go and everywhere you have been. Open your arms and your hearts out wide. Feel the love for you, each other and also from above, because we are all one and inseparable, always.

Imagine for a moment the simplest things. A duck and its egg about to hatch. The seed of a plant about to be sown on the wind. A fly or wasp flying high in the sky searching near and far, a child's outstretched hand, asking for? A badger foraging for it's young and the tree that drops it's fruit, it's seed, to go on. Where does it all begin? (PAUSE)

It all began with a flux, a strand of energy brought together by the Supreme Creator. It is knowledge, it is wisdom, can you comprehend? Over the millennium this strand of energy grew and grew. (Life as _you_ know it is like a click of a finger, a fragment of time and space - a dimension that man cannot really perceive as yet).

The seeds of life, nurtured and cradled with immense love, the most potent relationship you can ever imagine. No powers or restriction has ever been governed over you and no intervention of what right or wrongs you do - that is not the way you have been left to grow. However the time is coming (as we have said) to go and make your 'bed'. Will it be neat and smooth and comfortable or will you make it in a rush and a shambles?

This process of growth and renewal is your final destiny and is each of your own individual making. Shape it as you will - will it become the sweetest or bitterest pill? That is for each and everyone of you to decide; to look and nurture what is so deep inside. Open up your toughened shell, crack it open then go and tell.

The world is waiting to overcome its struggles and live in new freedom. A task so hard and difficult you are all needed to give love. If every individual cast their net (as has been said), the canopy of love will spread and spread. It can and will, if you decide to open each of your hearts and your religions in your minds.

They are but labels that someone has decided to give, 'Ah, yes that seems right' or 'right, that fits'. What a mistake after generation to generation, confusing and belittling the people of each nation. A collective mind or single motion hiding the truth from careful deliberation. Forcing an issue and saying, "They will follow me and all and sundry" when they set out to deceive for their own lives and for their own greed.

Everyone can decide for themselves what is right and what is wrong and those that fight with hand and gun will wish they can retract their mistake. But. . . is it too late if they've have already written on their slate? Etched their 'karma' forever and a day so when their physical body dies, they will learn that they have to pay. They may be left in darkness for a long time until they can show the 'creator' they have changed.

Think about this, "How long may that be?" A day, or for eternity? I can hear you thinking, David, "I'm glad that it is not me". They have no morals, just 'we' and fight to slaughter man and his child, his son and daughter. Their hate will turn to fear and you are right to think as you do. One day they will understand but will it be too late for them?

Okay, we do not mean to frighten anyone so we'll move on now to the love and the light which has begun and to reiterate the love and the light that awaits.

Tears of joy lie in wait for you with colours of love sprinkling down to fill your hearts with wondrous love and the beautiful light. You will step inside to so much love, so much love spinning around for all to see and you will all feel like children again, reconnected in the most wonderful way. (PAUSE)

Try to touch your soul, your spirit in a unique way; now think of your most happiest time or day. A mother giving birth to her child or a loved one returned who you thought was lost. A love for a pet you thought you would never find or the most treasured love (or PAIN) that you have inside. Multiply it by infinity and again and again and you may, just may, feel and understand what lies in wait. You have all got the chance to feel this love so unique from all around and above.

Learn to live and to trust. Embark on your own individual journeys across the land, the sky, the sea and 'inside' you will find the true you and the true me. A beginning for each of you with no end.

A circle of life and the truth is sent. So sow your seeds in whatever way you can by opening up your true hand. From simplicity itself in helping someone to cross the road, to helping the insect stuck on its back, is giving something of yourself. When you care, nothing, but nothing is unachievable. Group together and grow in strength.

Form bands of love and show you care. Walk hand in hand and keep truth in your hearts and then you will understand and will never part. Every single thing is part of you and each other. The molecule, the atom, the DNA and structure - you have been made as one and your 'rest of your life' has only just begun. A challenge, a task lies in the hand. . . will you grab it and make a sacrifice, or say that it is not mine to give or share or to lend. (PAUSE)

Time is drawing close again my son. A short while till we meet again. Keep trying to do the right things and other people will see and want to know more. One day at a time doing the best that *you all* can, to strive forward into love, hand in hand.

We are always with you, never ending love from us to you. Goodbye, my son. Love, truth, peace and me. . .

ME: Thank you Spirit and all my guides and teachers. Love from me to you, forever.

MONDAY 14th AUGUST 1995 9.00 a.m.

ME: Please Great Spirit and all of my family, friends, guides, teachers and ministers of healing (you are all part of me) so draw close. I need your protection, guidance, truth, strength and most importantly, your love: It feeds me and sustains me. We are one and I love you all with all of my heart. Please teach me to serve and help others.

May I ask. . .

a) For your continued teachings and to explain more of your name and where you come from and your line of 'ascension'.

b) My task on the Earth 'Plane'. You know all of what has happened in our 'circle', but I feel I need to do as much as I can with you *and* for the circle. I do not want you to think that I am separated in what I feel. We are one and everything is for the course of love and light to flourish. Please, please help us on the Earth plane. Let us see with your hope and love. Forever your son, David.

COMMUNICATION: We are here my son. Why do you worry when this frequency is here forever? We love you and we are one, always to be this way. You have asked for us to draw close again, Why? We have never been away and so shall it always be.

We think and see all of you all the time. When you laugh, when you cry and when you die it is the happiest time of all. For when you 'cross over' the feelings are so immense, the peace and the tranquillity, the one last fence. Not of barbed wire or brambles or of any pain, but of something that you cannot comprehend, as yet.

This is the love and the light that radiates so brightly, not blinding but is nourishment, the food of the heart. You will see, as all those that are ready to see when their time is right.

It is so good to be with you so you can learn and pass these messages on. One day at a time David. Patience, be patient. Your circle has and is going through a time of transition. Judy has been given a task to do and she will do it very well to learn and to tell. Yours is slightly different. Pathways are as we have already explained to you - no right or wrong way.

Go with your heart, we will not stop this frequency. It is yours and ours alone - a line of communication to us and our home. Steady my son, please concentrate as your love shines through. . .

We have said that we are from the Two Sisters Star Group and this is true. The line of Ascension you ask for, is this new for you? Where we reside is past the Bear, the Plough, and you will need fresh and different eyes to see us David. Look beyond the smallest of this constellation and slightly to the right and you will see the smallest flicker of light. This is our home of which there are two; not far apart but immense for you. We have one 'moon' similar to yours, a beautiful light shining by day and by night.

Why do we have two homes? The Creator gave us these for space for us to grow. Both of peace and a heavenly glow, no overcrowding and no distance and travel too much. We can go from one to the other by the slightest touch, speed of thought. Just like that, so easy. It is a wondrous thing that the Creator has given us.

Lines of Ascension - you are thinking of your earthly plane and 'he' who has gone before. Yes, we have had similar names and similar fates which lie in store to return to the light and so much more but we are not and never have been of your Earth plane.

You ask in your mind to describe what we are like. . . Huh, you bring a smile to me and those around - can your imagination really 'wonder' David? What we would like you to do in a few moments of time is to relax and 'drift'. David, come with us on a special trip, no fare to pay. (See, we can have and do have a sense of humour too!) Before we do, someone else would like to have a word with you. . .

Hi, David! It is the first time we have spoken. My name is 'Zerrog', spell it in your letters of your alphabet - how it sounds. Our words and communication is totally different but the Creator has taught us well in yours. I just wanted to say you are never alone and a friend of us, you will always stay. Please take our hand and come on this small journey. Relax and slow your breathing rate down.

Go ahead my son, you will know my name too soon enough. Put your pen down for a little while. (PAUSE)

ME: This was amazing. I drifted off so fast. I left England, over the sea, the Earth and into space. Past Stars, then the Plough and then a faint Star. Somehow I knew where I was going - the Two Sisters, the moon and into light.

Suddenly it felt like I was in a room surrounded by light yet sparkling around me were flickers of different light too. Somehow I was told 'they' have two densities, one of light and one of 'matter'. Everything was a little hazy as if my vision was not tuned in. Then I saw a figure come forward from the light. . .

I fully expect that some people reading this and seeing this next picture to think, or say "Made it up. Seen from a film. All in his mind, etc, etc". All I can say is that what I 'saw', felt and experienced and now describe to you is from my heart. I know this WAS a life form, an extra-terrestrial or NBE (Non-biological entity) and. . . a friend I knew. (What reason would I have to lie?) This 'being', my friend (and family) lifted his hand. A finger touched my hand and the most beautiful light flowed 'into' me. I then knew his name. . . 'Millanderer'. (Picture Eight: 'MILANDERER' Page29)

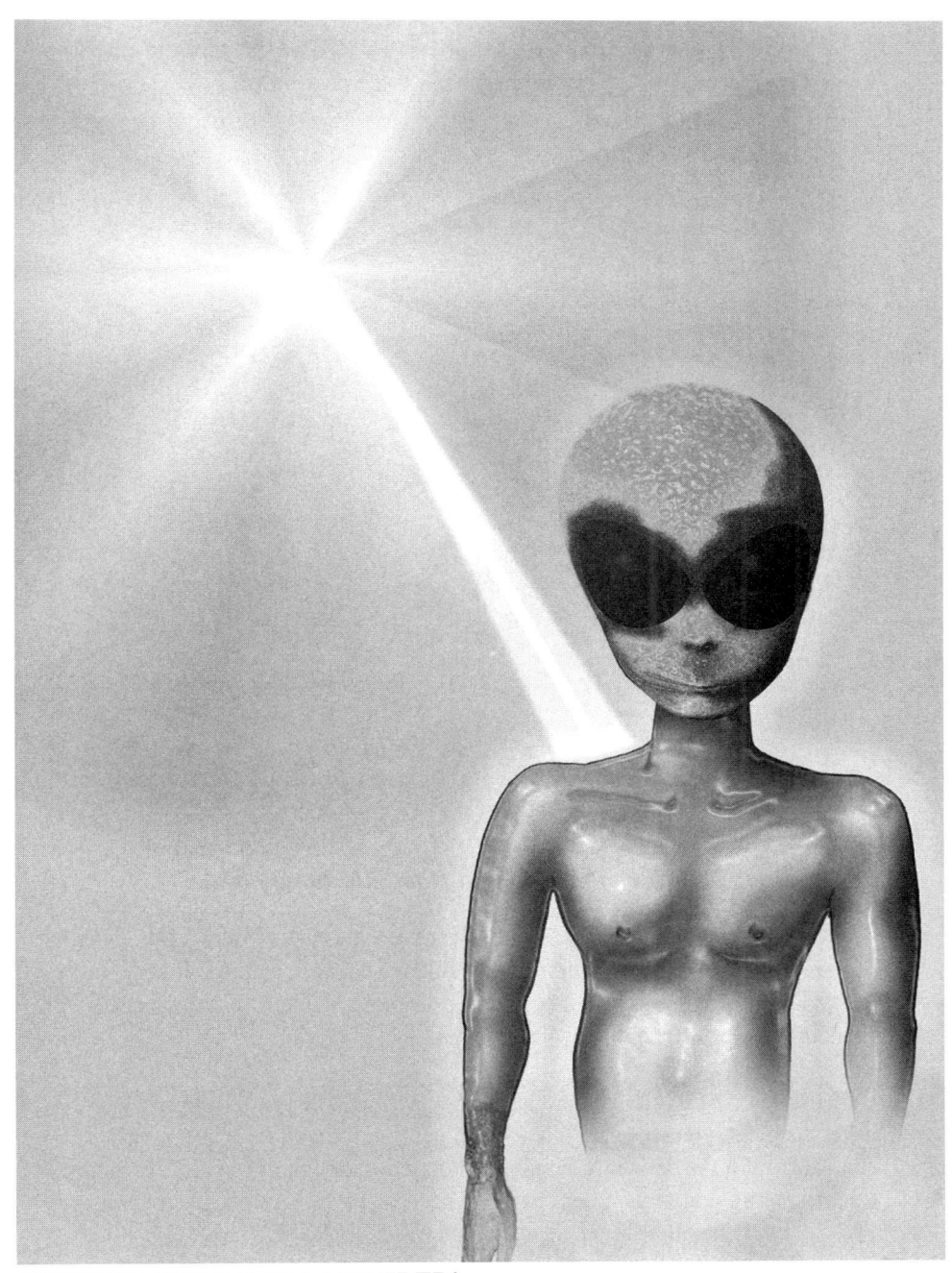

PICTURE EIGHT: 'MILLANDERER'

After this, I saw what looked like two doors which opened up to reveal some sort of large screen. . . in the distance was the planet Earth.

PICTURE NINE: 'VIEW SCREEN'

My line of sight/vision from this direction

I did not know or feel conscious of the time that 'passed' during this. Then I felt myself spinning downwards and I could see a flower and it was as if I just melted into it and flowed like energy through it back to the Earth. . . Wonderful!

COMMUNICATION: You are back now my son. The spark of love which I have just given you will give a boost and see you through to light up your life and shine all around. Leave no stone unturned upon your ground. Cast aside troubles, strife and fears - they have no need or place here. They are things you will overcome to lead others to become 'one'. (PAUSE)

As a rainbow bears across your land twisting and radiating it's colours like a magic wand the fragments of light sparkling in the rain means that mankind has the chance to begin again. The pot of gold at the end is not solid for man to gain and spend but is of love for all to share. A never dying source which comes from above.

Let the colours of your eyes that you perceive, the reds, the oranges, the yellows and greens heal again. Let the blues and mauve's that you sow begin to show and let the golden ray begin to say what is in your heart and the pure white light, light up your lives.

Many colours are for many different things and each on there own release a beauty and love that's way deep inside you to be let free for all to see. The pain and hurt of the deepest black radiates sickness and darkness of that which is the 'negative' and hidden bane part of you. Push it back with the brightest light every day and every night and let this envelope of beauty cast aside all your sins by pushing them into light. (A darkness before that festered and smelt of death, disease and greed. Those are things that you must now release.)

The rolling green fields and those of brilliant yellow and gold are the ones that can heal in the love and kindness and shining brightness for growth. The single nourishment that you all need to expand is the 'colour' of love to every land. Black or white, red or yellow, rich or poor, meek or mellow, the thin or fat, the clean or dirty, the well or ill, come on, all climb the hill.

Reach the top so you can see the valley below. Raising the light, it's embers to burn and glow. Walk into the light and make it brighter still and create the cord that is starting to be built of silver, gold and brilliant white light that climbs like a ladder deep into the night.

Climb, climb each rung of hope and faith and open your hearts still further each step that you take. Reaching the top is not too hard for many helping hands will give you a gentle push. A push not a shove from us or anyone, but a soft and gentle motion guiding you, helping you, when you need to grow - to expand in what you need to know. The lessons of joy and love will attract those who wish to grow and acknowledge that which opens up a new door for them. Helping them to sow and to help them spin the web of love to draw more and more light in. (PAUSE)

Well my son, time draws in your world for us to end with enough said today for you to grow and understand. You have caught a glimpse of our homeland and touched my hand too. David, you are indeed a true friend.

Be yourself, (as we have said before), just be yourself. You can do no more. Till we meet again and move closer towards our goal, keep strong, be tall and stretch out your hand to do the very best you can. Love from us to you *all*. We miss you so and till we and the other worlds are in tow and unison of being one, live life to the full, be one my son. Love, truth, peace and me. . . Goodbye.

ME: Bless you all. Today was so wonderful. I will become all that I can become. Love from me to you, always. Thank you.

CHAPTER TWO

'UNDERSTANDING'

WEDNESDAY 16th AUGUST 1995 10.00 a.m.

ME: To the Great White Spirit my guides, teachers and ministers of healing you are all of my family and friends (we are one).

On this frequency to my 'special family' and friends who share their love with me (THE TWO SISTERS STAR GROUP and Millanderer and Zerrog) I ask, "Do you channel yourselves *direct* with the Creator or through your mediums of light or sources? If so, who and what are they? Also, do you have friends on other planets like you who are helping others or are you unique?" So many questions I could ask you. . . I know you are close to me right now.

COMMUNICATION: Welcome again my son - so soon to write again and we are pleased when we feel your love coming through on this frequency. Such peace and stillness is needed that we must help and create it for humanity so that all can see, not just for you or for me.

The Light has and knows all things and when you become part of the light everything is there. The two bodies the Creator has given us enables us to become part of his light. When we are light we are his light and can know and be *anywhere* as we have already said. When we need an answer we immediately become light and it is there nurturing and loving us. It is so beautiful, so profound, never feeling lost or hurt and bound to Him in peace and love forever. A beautiful thought isn't it?

You see, we have no middle channel to go through and just like you and mankind are unique in every sense. One of a kind who has learnt by his mistakes and in time this knowledge will be revealed.

Yes, we have many friends and family that we have met along our way. Some very dear to our hearts and others that still have a long way to go in wisdom and knowledge to 'become' one.

Our task is to help them all, as many as possible, just like you. It is a wondrous feeling to help and watch the Creator's love grow and grow and for us to be part - just a small part - of that which he has sown. We will tell you more of our friends when the time is right but it is not fair on them or you, right now.

We can hear your many questions inside your mind. Please be patient David, one day at a time. Everything at its natural pace. We would not wish to rush you before you are ready as this forms part of your 'understanding'.

This 'UNDERSTANDING' is the second chapter's title David. The first chapter's name is (was) for you to decide. A beginning, an end, a circle, a friend? Feel from your heart and the title will start. (PAUSE)

We last spoke of the colours and spectrum of light and lighting up your night. Today we need to let you know how these fit in and glow within everything.

Imagine if you will, a small nut on a tree. What is it made of? Particles, chemicals and vitamins containing life force and nourishment and sometimes encased in a shell. It lives and feeds from a 'connection' to the tree, it's 'mother', it's love and food from the land and from the sky.

In a similar way you, (mankind) is like a nut. 'He' has a body (a shell) and different layers of 'body' to which of course many people know. The Astral/ the Etheric and so forth but your true self is the nut inside to be nourished from the light source. A true being in every sense, made of energy at no expense. Your true selves are beautiful to see, not dense or thick, but of the most fascinating existence that could be. Your true self is attached to the life force - the tree - by fragments of light infinitely long.

The Creator has housed your 'selves' well so that you may learn and feed, not in a physical sense (of course you do need that) but of the *light*. By taking in the light of truth and of love it helps to cleanse and give this nourishment that you all need to have within yourselves. It feeds and sustains your very being. Without love and truth you die and not just in the physical sense either.

When the nut is released from the tree, just like a seed, it floats in the wind and it comes to rest. It is nurtured till it grows itself. A simple principle isn't it? The shell is broken and withers away when the time is right for it's rebirth to the light.

Sometimes the wind blows the seed, the nut, where it cannot see and it shrivels and distorts itself into an ugly mess. These are the seeds, the people and light that has chosen to bury itself in the darkness and spread decay and disease to those around. What we need to do is to cut this disease back, all around and get the light to those shrivelled shells because they are still part of you and me and of the Great Spirit - The Creator.

If we do not, they will be 'lost' *forever*. The task is not just our own and is down to those that we speak of to want to flourish and grow and to find their true 'selves' and their true home. The tree that has given birth to all these seeds has new work to do as always and has, if it wants to, to stop bearing the fruit and the nut - if ways are not changed.

If the sun moves around and nourishes the other side of the tree, it is down to each and everyone of you to follow and still live and learn in the light. Those that remain who stick and flounder in the bad ground may not be found and nurtured but will groan, never, (maybe) to find their way home. A simple tale for those to understand, wouldn't you agree?

So, the particles and minute fragments of life nurtured from the tree is you and me and everything. But we do not need to go into 'compositions' and of the 'ingredients' because we doubt that it is time yet for mankind to comprehend this - yet. You are still learning DNA and structures of this kind but there is growth way beyond this that makes up you and all mankind. One day perhaps . . . there is a phrase:

"Life - light - the truth indeed, be one - be free - no greed.

Give not take to make progress, in your hearts, love address.

Choices to make and chances to be made, give love and be true to yourself . . . do not be afraid.

I am you and you are me, return with love to the tree".

We do not have to send complicated messages for you all to understand as you have the choices and means to hand. Feel the beauty deep within and take your own hand and shape your own destiny. The light is brighter than a billion suns but is never blinding. The love so amazingly beautiful - oh, we wish that you all could see.

Life for you is precious we know but open your hearts and do not turn your backs. The journey is only hard if you make it that way, "Oh dear! what will I do - what will people say?" Why worry, if you know the truth and feel it in your heart.

The fickleness in other hearts is something that you must break and cast aside. Break the shell in two and then let the true 'you' inside grow with the beautiful light every day and every night as you sleep and as you wake. Make your bed in happiness and let others be drawn in peace and love.

Hold their hand and side by side carry them through life to laugh and cry through both the good and bad times. Do your best and see them through, show the love you have (the true you) thats 'connected' to each of us by strands of love.

David, time is drawing in again. Others will learn and have their say, teach them these messages and love the Creator's way. Till next time, my son, goodbye we say. Love, truth and peace from me and us. Always.

ME: Thank you from my heart to my family and my friends forever.

SATURDAY 19th AUGUST 1995

ME: I'm hoping to hear you again today with your loving words of light and truth which nourish me. It is so hard to describe each time a droplet of 'everything' flows through me and my 'self'. Such love and understanding in which I flower with joy and open my arms and heart to new thinking.

I am one with you all and ask to serve the Great Spirit (the Creator) in love and light and to fulfil my destiny on this earth plane. May I ask. . . How old is your civilisation? How far in 'earth time' (as in our perception of it) are we away from you?

What is the next page too? I am so excited at receiving you it fills my heart with anticipation. You are my family, my friends and are part of me forever.

COMMUNICATION: As you look upon the night sky we hear the many wondering. . . why? So much can happen even in the time of a blink of an eye. You are right again to perceive the distance only in your terms. The time physically it would take you to reach us, as your technology stands at this present time, is immense. Light years 10 x 10 x 10.

Mankind may one day really be able to comprehend this and be ready. Who knows? Many questions and many burning hearts and so much information for us to part with David but you must be patient for it my son - eager as you are.

Our roots have grown for a long time, millions of years longer than when mankind first existed. Born of light in a similar way but fed different light and hence we have grown in a different way. We reproduce and have evolved very differently - again all explained at a later date. We can tell you that many species have called us by many different names; some flattering, and don't laugh, some not so!

There is no benchmark for age like your earth plane, AD and BC etc., it does not exist and never has for us. Time and distance has no real fruitfulness for us, although we have things and schedules to complete - our tasks in hand. However, we do not look at a clock face and think of having too little or too much to utilise. Sometimes it would be nice to see mankind working with their flow and natural culmination, rather than getting from A to B as fast as you can. . . What does it achieve? How does that fit in with the overall plan?

At the same time we know you all have needs to meet and the way you live and the need for heat for example. We do not have cold and hot or go to see what is in the pot. Some of you might say, "Is that not boring?" We would say this to those of that opinion. . . when you are light and in the light of the Creator, you do not have a need for anything as we have sustained life and energy as we have already explained.

You wish to ask our people's name, well think of this as a little game David. We are not messing about, but wish to see if you can discover. . .

What would you do in a sea so blue?
What would you do if you cried and died?
Where the sun and the horizon meet, do the reds and blues compete?

A shining light on a silver surface, glistening in your mind,
now trace back the steps to find one of a kind.
Is it a name that comes to the surface?
If in doubt do you shout?

If a tear falls do you feel big or small?
If life's a real bitch, is it time for worship?
Here in a 'symbol' you will know our name,
hoped you like our little game.

Okay David, let's start today with a new page and a story of great age. Inspired and trusted for generations and generations as we expanded in knowledge and attained wisdom.

Our forefathers of our civilisation came together to watch and listen to each of our nations. "Be one" they cried and "Lift your hearts and voices so that many more can see." Let them judge for themselves what they can see and hear. An indentation of hearts of steel, barricaded in prejudice and hate and the raw deal. "Lift your arms up" was said and "cast them out wide, holding a hand of friendship with whoever next to you resides."

A circle united for eternity is now watching over all. The clean and the dirty, rich or poor, black or white, it makes no difference in the circle of light.

Please know that a shooting star is a 'calling' from afar and a comet's speed* is to show your real need. So overcome any distance in your hearts to show the real you, not only the part that cries out for more to light up your shore. One by one there is a new beginning - a fear, a trial and events to overcome one by one.

David, you are so physically tired whilst sitting here you drift into near sleep state and your frequency changes.

ME: I felt so tired but I pulled myself together.

COMMUNICATION: (Contd.) There will come a day when each and everyone agrees to their needs to see the joy and life without pain. A new dawn and a new era explained to those that open their eyes and seek.

When a friend or family is in distress, what do you feel or how do you react - with a guiding hand or a stab in the back? Has your brother or sister done something wrong? Are your uncle and aunty apart as they don't get along?

Who is 'closer', a friend, a father, a mother, a child, a son or daughter? Each a different feeling and a different love that is in your hearts that comes from the Creator above and not to be played (ever), against one or another.

Can you or anyone describe and understand the love that entwines and encases and bonds you all together? What is love?

---

*Comet's speed:- I wondered . . . perhaps a special name would be given to a brilliant light that will light up our night?

WHAT IS LOVE?

Is it tangible? Is it right? Is it wrong? What is love?
Is it energy, is it yours or ours alone?
Does it stop and start or forever part?
Can you see or hear the gap in place,
that needs to be filled by all of the human race?

When you cry and the tears flow from your eyes,
how many times have you asked, "Please God Why?"
Why this pain and the feeling of hurt deep inside?
How can you do this God? Why have you gone to hide?

You could have saved him or her or my best friend,
why didn't you Father?   Why did you not explain this
danger and the risk and the need to take care?
When they left me this morning without touching my hand,
I never told them I loved them, or ran my fingers through their hair.

Now they are gone and I can't turn the clock back.
Why my God, could you not keep them on the right track.?
If you could have helped them why did you not?
Alone now am I as I sit in my chair; do I rot?

Father, dear Father, I do not understand love, the love you have
given and taken away from me,
As I sit and stare and look out to the deep blue sea.
I'm so empty and all I see is the sea, sky and nothing for me for miles around,
only images and ghosts of the past, reflecting in my soul and my heart abound.

The pain and anguish of them floating away, nothing but memories now in me
they'll stay.
And as I bare my heart to you Father, and you now listen to me,
I would sacrifice everything that you have given to love them again.
Suddenly now in my darkest hour, I feel like death has overtaken my life, . . .
no power,

Then, in my mind a distant bright light, beneath a small tree I see.
Where is it? What is it?   And I race to thee.
A beautiful captivating pull of my heart,
and inside the light I see everything, in clouds and in parts.

Of life, my friends and those that I have lost today,
and for a brief second I taste the love that I have never known.
Now I understand Father that you care and are everything,
in a lesson that love, pure love is never lost or thrown.
I know that my love has not gone at all,
but has passed into the light, that you have set aside for all.

Forgive me Father, my God, the Great Spirit,
sometimes I am weak but also have grown with it.
Love is a special, precious, wonderful feeling,
that can't be explained by anyone or anything.

You are Love beyond a shadow of a doubt and I know this in my
heart and my very soul.
And today in my despair and such seeming of loss,
you have carried me, trusted me, held me and I am no longer lost.
One day I will touch their hand and stroke their hair,
now I have seen the light and true love, will I ever again despair.

ME: I had this thought. It was as if the poem was from someone else and their love, pain and joy was for us all, as 'one'.

COMMUNICATION: David, What is love? Love is everything, everything is love. The Creator's strongest force, never broken but sometimes entwined. The line of love is eternal for everyone. Open all your hearts and become still, be one with the Creator's love for you all.

Love my son is a wondrous thing so dry your tears and have a rest, you are one. Till we talk again, try to have some fun in your heart and in ours we know what you said. We are one forever, forever my son. Goodbye in love, truth, peace and me.

ME: Feelings that I have never experienced before, a joy, a love for me. I feel an overwhelming spark in my heart ignite now and a fire which glows throwing a light so bright up to you on the different planes and dimensions. You are my family and friends and my love is so immense for you all and the Great Spirit only you can ever know. For me, love is you and everything that the Great Spirit flows through you. Goodbye for now.

ME: (Contd. from original notes. From the communication on Saturday 19th August 1995.)

The little 'game' fascinated me and I wouldn't be telling you the truth if I didn't say it frustrated me. I kept thinking, it must be so 'simple' yet I must be making it hard for myself. Over and over in my mind I tried to decipher each line and each meaning.

Swim	Rejoice	I kept coming up with
Yes	Moon? Light	different words etc.
Jesus - Lord	Prayer	Things like these here:-
Infinites?	Lantions?	Landtions?
Symbols . . .	This is the wrong direction I thought.	

I kept thinking 'I'm trying too hard to know this and for a couple of days just kept on *wondering* about it.

TUESDAY 22nd AUGUST 1995 9.55 a.m.

ME: To all my friends and family, the Great Spirit and light bearers and light carriers on every plane of existence.

Please only communicate in truth, love, light and in peace. I am one and am 'still' for your frequency of wisdom and knowledge. I am here to serve the Great Spirit and to help those in need.

Please, my family and friends from the Two Sisters Star Group - your little riddle you sent me - please do not think I want it easy. I will and want to work hard but can you let me have another clue to your name? I will and do understand why you want me to do this search within. Love to you all in the short time together today.

COMMUNICATION: The frequency is strong again my son and we understand your many needs. Words of wisdom and knowledge and love is everywhere around, you (and all) just need to look for it is there to be found. As rain falls down the window pane and the sun beats down to grow the grain, life and nourishment is for everything from outside and within.

Okay, my son, more information for you - to be one today and for always.

Many different routes, what will you take?
Left, right or straight on to know,
or a backwards step into darkness you will go?
The blues and the reds are one of light,
And the riddle you talk of is only in the mind,
Aren't you and I one of a kind?
The glistening light on a shining surface.
Is the light of your heart radiating through your mind,
across the surface - the Earth plane of mankind?
If you cried and died, what would you do?
Would you be feeling cold or blue?
No. You would be in the land of joy, truth and light,
happiness not sadness all around, your spirit and soul taking flight.

What would you do on a sea so blue? Wouldn't you travel and be in touch with the elements. The sky, the sea and when you came to rest on land, light a fire to warm your hands? A destination , a foreign land to discover and cultivate in love and peace.

As we go through your mind and you now say 'symbol' - what shape do you have in your head? This symbol has no edges or corners David (another clue), remember some of the things we can do. We have said we have come to help you all, through the Creator's guidance. Travel, light, love, peace and truth, nurturing and helping both one of a kind. See if you can get closer to the name from the extra information.

This is the part of your individual growth. Look beyond the top layer of everyday things to that below, David. So many people take so, so many things at face value. Scratch the surface and dig deep to the core. Therein you will find the truth and a whole lot more for you to share and to say out loud to both the individual and to the large crowd.

When a gathering is drawing close speak of being 'one' not individuals. Create the light, and the harmony that fits people. When they put their hands in their gloves or their foot in their shoe, they know it is their own because it feels good. It fits right, is not too loose or not too tight. When knowledge and wisdom, love and truth touches their hearts, they will know when it is time for them to try this new 'fit' - this new glove, this new shoe and only when they are ready will it feel right for them. Some will need to grow fast but will join in time, to knit together and become one. Some will understand straightaway, some will need to learn another day. (PAUSE)

This is just a short message today David my son, other things and your work to be done. Speak to you again soon, take care. You will learn, so never despair. Love to you from us all in love, truth, peace and me.

42

WEDNESDAY 23rd AUGUST 1995

ME: I kept going over and over the 'extra information' in my mind and on notepaper, jotting down and deciphering the messages, remembering not to try too hard and to look beyond the 'surface' of each line and meaning.

Light	-	one of a kind	
Doubt	-	shout	
Symbol	-	not physical - no curves or edges	
Elements of one			LIGHT
Travel			LANTERN
Over land and sea	-	Infinite	
	-	Space - TRANS	ACROSS
		ABOVE/BELOW	OVER
			IN/OUT

I still didn't seem to be nearer yet also had a feeling that I was 'getting there'.

FRIDAY 25th AUGUST 1995 10.30 a.m.

ME: Dear Great Spirit and all my friends and family on all the different planes of existence, we are together in love and light - never divided.

As I become still, I hope to receive your guidance, strength, peace and wisdom and to touch your love even greater each time we meet in these quiet times. I only wish to serve and to help others. To guide them in your name and for understanding.

Many things I could ask for but I only wish to reaffirm our love and light as always. Please during this time, feel my love and light that I send to you. Even though you are 'here', I miss you so much.

COMMUNICATION: We are here again my son, to teach and to nurture you as always. Oh, my son, we (all) ask for progress for you all, to attain the best you can become. To be all one, as you said, in peace and harmony. As we watch and see the daily activities on your world and feel the pain, we try and try to send our love but often in vain. With what we are trying to achieve with you, and others working and completing their tasks too, we hope to spread the light so brightly so that all can see (as we have said before). (PAUSE)

Time to continue David, to another page and this is centred around mistrust (mistrust and trust). Words divided by just a few of your letters, but also divided by huge chasms of hurt, pain and of love.

Many people do not trust each other and often in your world it is easy to understand why this is so. Those that do trust each other and those that trust from within have completely different lives and outlooks. What we hope to say and explain today is to bridge this gap a little, to explain this pain and dissolve it from people's hearts and minds.

To love we must trust. To trust ourselves and the feelings we have inside. We must all trust the feelings inside before we can show others trust or even explain or grow in trust.

Trust is simple, trust is love and peace and harmony. Trust starts within yourself to become one with the 'Source', the Creator. People must learn the simple fact that when someone has a feeling of pain or joy and there is an ache so deep inside . . . tears fall. Tears from the heart and a pain so immense that you cannot explain and you often do not know what to say. Why? Because a tear says it all.

When there is a trust in that all things are meant to be and are of a learning process you can then start to learn to live in a proper way. I do not mean something simple like brewing a drink of tea or making the bed, cleaning the windows or fixing a shelf in the shed but major events and the things that the individual needs to overcome and to understand.

Let things 'go' in your heart and things become simple and are made simpler to understand. These obstacles and feelings that bring despair with physical words are side events to detract and test, to see if you can overcome them.

Trust in the good in all things that are said and done (Not easy by any means in the way you all live). Some things of course will not come out to your advantage or liking but what lessons have been learned along the way? To forgive, to let go, to share, to relax or in despair, love, hate to overcome becoming daily closer to the One?

Everything is so simple if you stop and think of someone else's feelings and someone else's cares and not just your own. 'Me, me, me' is what so many think. 'Can't do that if it's not good for me' or 'Can't do that if I don't gain in some way'. (In a material sense). That is all so dense and so dark it leads to distrust and hate for one another and putting the divide, this wedge, deeper and deeper and it is harder to break free.

When someone has a feeling of utter dejection and complete loss, what do they really feel? - Alone and cold, lost? How can you turn that around and come closer to the truth? Why did that happen - that event that changed my life? Why wasn't it better for me in the outcome? Why was he/she so against me in my desires? Why did that child go and let down my tyres? - A joke or a truth - simple to understand. To delay you or to get you to change the way you are and how do you feel and think?

When things do not go your way, do you think 'Why me?' Or just think *why?* Search within and feel what you have learned from the day and the message it brings. When you are awake and when it 'registers' while you are asleep - subconsciously, things are etched within yourself and the learning process increases as you go along and one by one the things you overcome.

TRUST

Inside is you and your soul, your spirit and your mind,
learning to live and to trust yourself and mankind.
Things go wrong, they often do, causing anger of 'red' and feelings so 'blue'.
Boiling point of no return? Or a relapse to find a new PATHWAY home.

To trust your feelings and intentions of love for one another,
are branches you extend to your sister or your brother.
The tree of life and evolution everlasting, does it matter you're a pauper or a
past or future king?

Who is right in love and peace? The man that hates and mistrusts one and
everything, or he who gives and shares and learns to trust within.
Mistrust or trust are two destinies and desires of your hidden feelings,
so relax the one true you, to try a new beginning.

Outstretch your hands and embrace all living things,
and trust in the good, the learning and experiencing.
In this your lifetime, this time around,
lift off from the darkness and the black on the ground.

Opening your hearts and embrace those all around,
to fly high in the light of both the day and the night.
Your wife, your husband, your children, your family are all bound,
so trust in them and yourself for then you'll all be found.

Push aside negative feelings and overcome the darkness and be aware,
do not mistrust *and show that you don't care.*
You all are one and in trust become still,
do this and don't struggle but please all climb this hill.

One by one, reach the top and look at what you see,
the love, the peace, the light and the true harmony.
All one frequency and of the same united dimension,
the learning and growing in waves of understanding. . . towards the one true
heaven.

Simple choices really, and they are down to the individual - to live by what they do and say. Please, please try harder than ever before. Go deep down right to your core of yourself and open your new door to unveil your new understanding and so much more of life.

David, now a little message we hope you will understand. Close your eyes right now and as a ray of light is sent, you will see it in your mind. (Picture Ten: A RAY OF LIGHT Page 47) . . . (PAUSE)

Lift up your frequency even higher still - this is important too just as the 'why and how' you feel. A friend has spoken much truth yesterday* and you must understand them. . . and 'feel' them, just as my hand is so so close and lays on your shoulder and you feel it making you warmer.

Discuss and sharing is important my son, but do not lower your frequency. David, you must always continue to reach for the stars, always teaching from within and afar. Those that understand will understand and still remain your close friends and this will give them a chance to also improve. True pathways are not manufactured or pushed together, but surface within (as always) bringing in light and casting out sin. Communication with others is always okay as long as it does not distract or lead to decay.

Your pathway as you know is a long, long road and you must make it easier for yourself by letting go (at least for the time being) to let yourself and others grow. Understanding is growth and growth is understanding as all things - a circle, never ending.

Relate on and to the truth and the light everlasting. Complete your destiny and your lifetimes making. Be one as always my son. Love and light forever from us always, in love, truth, peace and me. ('PS' our name - is in the 'Game'.)

ME: To you all from my heart. Thank you so much, I learn every time I'm with you and I grow and always know that you are me and I am you - one of a kind and one of light. Love from me to you all.

WEDNESDAY 30th AUGUST 1995

ME: To all my family and friends, I miss you even though you are here!

I ask today only for your guidance and continued assistance to serve the Great Spirit, the Creator. I am here to serve and open my heart and very being only to truth, love and light. I love you all.

---

*I went to see Lizz, my friend, a crystal healer (and she's so much more!).

PICTURE TEN: A RAY OF LIGHT

COMMUNICATION: Oh, my dear son. We see and know what is happening in all your lives and feel for you when the things that you think of go against you and upset you and your heart. Listen to the flow of things. Let your feelings go and turn within as you well know. Everything will be okay.

There is so much to go through and learn today so be strong and pull away from misgivings and any weaknesses. David, today is the last part of Chapter Two which is quite short and today we need to inform you of the flow of life and energy from the Creator, your Great Spirit God.

There have been many different names given by many different cultures and continents over many of your earth centuries of existence. One thing that is constant within them all is the fervour and strength of believability that has been created.

If only mankind could have harnessed their diverse and widened views and channelled them for love and peace and harmony as one. Perhaps today we would be looking at global peace and not all the conflict that seems to hit every beach, every shore of even the tiniest island and it's people. As has been said before, 'if only' but you have all progressed in the different ways and this is what also makes you individuals at the end of the day.

The strength of all of your beliefs could have been harvested if people of the different 'eras' in time had expressed that desire to do so rather than the greed taking over their minds and very beings. This has on many occasions of course, led to their destruction, their people's destruction.

This has happened way, way before your 2000 BC etc., and on many different planes of existence, so we are not pointing a finger at you in particular and condemning you. Everything that you and mankind has ever experienced has been for progress but it would be so much further advanced within technology and in harmony (which of course is more important). If only the leaders and controllers of society (and the people) had been nurtured or grown in a different way.

Now let us explain about this flow in more detail to you. Many people have said thought is action and thought is deed but there is so much more for you all to understand about the power of the mind and what it can do. One of the Creator's greatest achievements is the immense complexity of you and your species - so many facets and so many feelings.

Have you, (or has anyone) just paused for a moment and really thought how wonderful you are. To be able to think and feel and use the senses as you do. Marvellous, created by love (that is for sure) and people do not realise that they could do so much more (for and with these) to help each other and their fellow 'man'.

It is time to all expand the perceptioning and feeling of 'intuition', an energy and impulse sometimes hidden deep within. Open up your minds to these most strong energy patterns and feelings. Many more people will then understand so much more to their lives and existence and how they fit in with their overall pathway and destiny that they have chosen and embarked upon. When you turn within, cords or fluxes of spiralling energy (which cannot be seen by your physical eye) flow and glow brighter and brighter.

By opening up these channels or 'senses' beyond your normal '5', you are linking into the overall source of energy and very essence of yourself - the movement and the information and the light and love that is present in everything, swirling and swirling in unique patterns and fluxes.

When they can be seen it is a truly wonderful sight. Many different 'feelings' and colours and vibrations of energy are in fact just 'pure'. Even hard for us to observe sometimes. It is this 'pureness' that sustains everything and feeds and nourishes your very existence.

A source infinite which cannot and never will diminish. It is time for you *all* to perceive and to think so much more differently to what you do at the present. So much 'dense and baseness' all around with only pockets of light to be found. (PAUSE)

Imagine for a moment a blackened room (the darkest and deepest black). In each corner a flicker of light, four small candles burning bright. They have been lit for many many years but have almost been extinguished many times. Read into that what you will (think from the heart).

By expanding each of your individual thoughts and feelings you can each enter this darkened room, a fragment of time and space, a fifth dimension. By bringing in love and peace and adding to the light, you can link to each other and form a <u>new</u> light. What can be achieved is all your destinies and the light that can be everlastingly seen could be so immense it could unveil the deepest corner and shadow and give birth to such brightness and eternal understanding.

As each person and each group and each community links together and has felt and touched the energy that is with and around them, they can expand and grow in all directions. If, after a period of your time, growth is sustained and new 'candles' are in place, you may find four more in the room, one on each side.

Now, when these lights burn so brightly they can interconnect and form lines of information and pathways for others to follow. The cords of wisdom and existence. (David you seem confused for a moment, but you will understand as we move along). Remove the box (the room) to 'picture' the eight candles. Now draw four 'in and in' on your mind. The shape may represent many things but only one of a kind. A star perhaps and a glow so beautiful. Whatever *you* feel within. (Picture Eleven: FORMING THE LIGHT   Page 50)

49

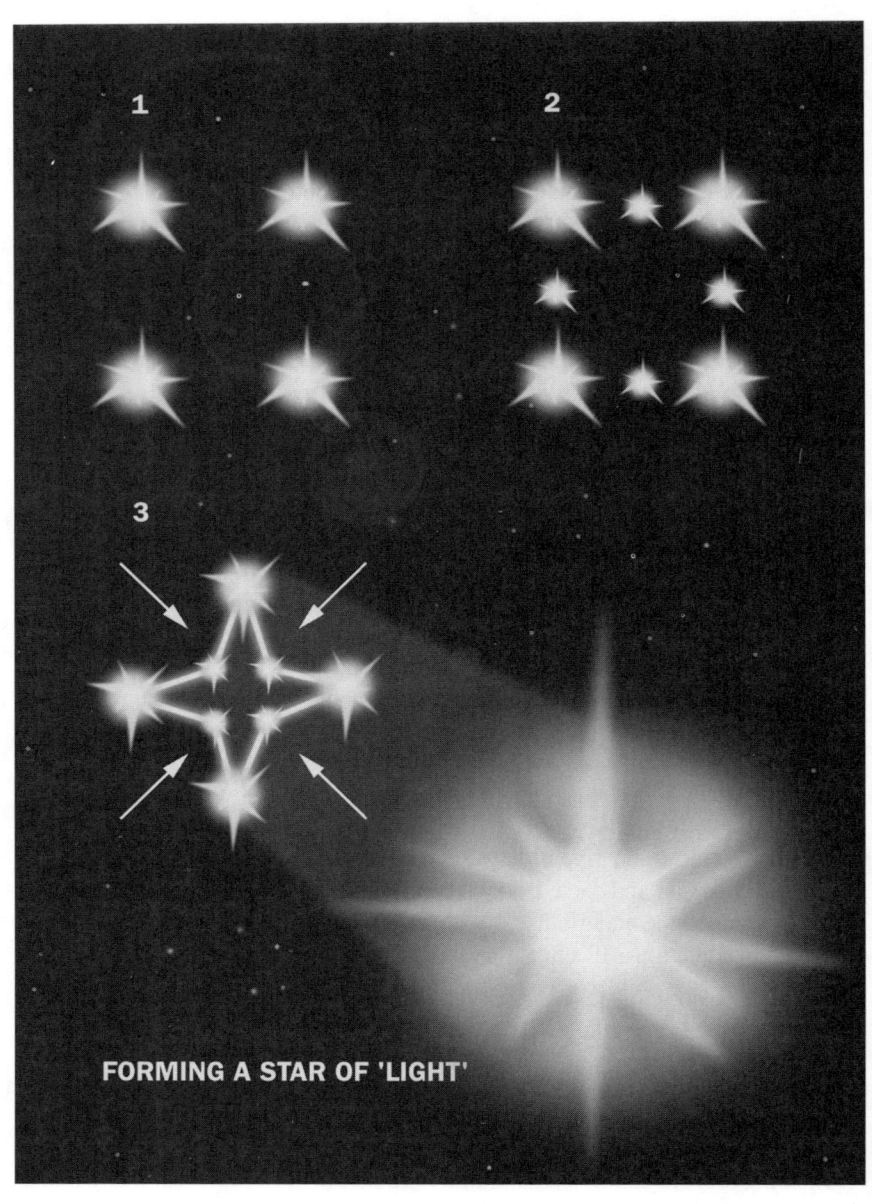

PICTURE ELEVEN: FORMING THE LIGHT

The point we are trying to make is that you yourself can choose what shape you make. You can choose what destiny to take - to live or to break. To be as many years before, misguided and in the room of darkness or to join each other in love and light not to be discarded. Here is a poem of the flow and your need to open up your other senses and to grow.

ENERGY AND FLOW

Energy and flow from no beginning and no end,
the understanding and the knowledge is inside to comprehend.
A flow, a constant flux, within and all around,
in each of your true 'self's, your soul and hearts are bound.
When joined together. . . more priceless than diamonds, pearls or gold,
God's love and light and energy, cannot be bought or sold.
ESP and travel, two fragments of the mind,
is it only for the few or for all of humankind?
Everyone divided and concerned to grow and learn,
but don't venture in to darkness for there's no return to home.

Touch and feel, the energy within and all around,
as you walk and also run with your feet that touch the ground.
As the wind blows through your hair, and a breeze that cools your face,
from the land of love and light, to help teach the human race.

Feel the energy and the flow which comes to you within,
one of your heart, your mind, your soul and of your true being.
Feeling of love and energy that gives and sends light in,
your heart. . . rejoice in peace, life eternal not for sin.

ME: N.B: As this was coming through, my mind strangely felt as if it was wandering.

COMMUNICATION: David, you must try harder to maintain the frequency. When your physical self is tired, do not try to push or pursue - let things be natural and tell us so if you feel you have to stop or need to go.

Well, Chapter Two David, comes to a close and we hope a few more 'people' will understand and will grow. Chapter Three is next in line to begin (when your pen is ready another time) and this will be entitled **'LESSONS'**. We hear you think, 'Intriguing'. . . and 'what next? It contains information that goes back to. . . Well, you'll just have to wait and see, my son.

We feel your love that you send each day David and your speck of light as you close your door to sleep at night. We hear your prayers and see your healing hands and light that you send. Never ever, lose your faith of what you comprehend and what you learn to live and love as you sleep in your bed. Everything in your time you just wait and see, we are one in truth and peace and in harmony. Till next time my son , all our love to you from us.

P.S: Read the 'Game' a few more times. Try to understand more to find our name and you will succeed - Love, truth, peace and me.

ME: Such emotion and as my tears fall I have felt your peace and tranquillity. I touch my heart and lift my hand for you to see. Not asking for more or to plead for anything, but to send my love, my light and my energy to thee.

You are part of my very existence and I will never, ever, ever forget these wonderful times we have had and will have together.

Till next time in love and light. Goodbye. David.

CHAPTER THREE

'LESSONS - 1, 2 AND 3'

MONDAY 4th SEPTEMBER 1995

ME: I pray and seek truth, love and your guidance as always for me to progress and to serve the Great Spirit, the Creator and all on this Earth plane. I open our special frequency for love and light to shine as always. May 'lessons' begin. . . (Parts 1,2 or 3?)

COMMUNICATION: Welcome again my son. Each of our hearts and arms are opened wide to share love and light and to give and seek 'love' in all things. It is time for worry and need to be cast aside during this time that you and 'us' have set aside. We will describe and mention just a few things today but you are right, the lesson will continue for us all. Today we start Chapter Three and as we have said, this will be broken down into three parts. Why? This will be explained and revealed. Let's start with the first part. . .

So much to learn then, lessons for life and beyond. Some easy and some that you haven't or cannot comprehend as yet.

In the beginning of time, many lessons were learned and experience gained in 'understanding' from many, many civilisations on many planets and in many galaxies. There was a 'searching period' that the Creator put forward for all species. A sort of initial concept or challenge for everything to perceive and learn. Many chose to turn their backs and go their own way - some initially quite successful but in the 'end' of their time, destructive to themselves.

Many, many earth years ago, mankind was born of light and consciousness and has evolved many times - not just over the fragment of time you call the last few thousand years. The earth has followed suit to some of this destructiveness three times before and is about to enter it's fourth time, another lesson.

It is approaching this very fast and this time those who succeed in their 'task' of love and light will expand beyond their physical 'selves'; (part of this has already been covered before, but we felt the need to reiterate this to you all).

The species, civilisations and planets that succeeded went on to learn and progress and enter (what we call) the middle phase/lesson and in a way, mankind (a very small part of it) is going through this stage. A continued search within themselves and everything around them and by using the other senses (as we have described before) to continue their expansion into light. Other planets evolved to this stage too, not to dissimilar to your own - and *failed*. Unfortunately to start afresh, 'anew', again.

It is now that this period of learning that so many (in billions of worlds) are going through with similar tasks to yours. This need to bridge the last gap and final hurdle to the last, but never ending 'learning' stage. One of beauty and splendour with peace, love and harmony, fully linked together as one.

In a sense it is a beginning - (a birth,) a middle - (a gathering or growing cycle) and the end - (to no end). This is the way that everything has always been and nothing, absolutely nothing can ever, ever detract from this. It is only when the species and the civilisations have reached the right and correct stage that the final beautiful, never ending journey can begin. Let us change tracks for a moment.

Many many teachers on your world (past and present) have decreed rules and judgements for the people of many different cultures and nations. Looking back into history, (and this is going to be quite controversial to some and not intended to be a whipping stick by any means), you have things like rules and legislations, guidance and understanding.

For instance, let us take the ten commandments and what they have taught the people who followed them. Back in those days, that era, people needed guidance to bring them back on line to become more 'holy' - but what is 'holy'? Can you or anyone define that?

This sustained part of your world for many years but it was like a straight-jacket in a way and tied many people's thoughts behind their backs and stopped people thinking for themselves. There are many truths (don't get us wrong) in each of the ten but what many failed to perceive was their own free will and destinies.

Life is a lesson and a learning process and each of you that are now ready to accept or to achieve their final destiny will understand this and of what we mean. What is right or wrong? Only the individual can tell themselves that. Shall I let free, or kill? Should I love or turn my back?

Every single decision that affects someone else is down to that individual - not some rule or instruction written in stone. Deep within your soul, your spirit, your very being is every answer that you need.

We are not, as just said, trying to antagonise or say, "Hey! You are wrong", but to question why and what you follow and have done so for so long. Whether it is being Christian, Catholic, Muslim, Hindu or following any particular religion that has been boxed or has been fashioned by one or more particular person.

Some leaders of all of these have indeed been very special and of those that are again on the earth plane at this present time have a very important role to play in bringing peace and harmony.

Let us look at just a few. We started with Christians and lessons. Jesus was a very, very gentle and loving man, placed at that particular time. A fantastic communicator and presence which gave an aura of love so far around.

What He tried to achieve was to turn you all to love and peace but did *not* at any time dictate or decree or tie hands behind backs. The way was left open for all to turn to the light, if and when ready to do so. He was indeed what you call a very 'old' soul *even then*. The Creator placed something within His spirit, His soul, that enabled Him to be what He was. . . and still is.

You see, 'still is'. This is because when born to the light you never leave it, as you are 'one'. This is what every single person forgets or does not know yet. He had tremendous ability to link with the light and could do the lessons He did this way. There were no miracles though and never have been - only truth distorted by mankind. Things were done and always have been by 'natural laws' and events occurred through the expansion of God's love, this is the 'MIRACLE' itself.

Many lessons in this beginning (i.e., this time around) have still a long way to go but can and will be achieved by those necessary to do so. (We could go so much more into detail but at this moment it is not required or necessary for us to do this).

Following truth, love, peace and harmony is not hard, difficult or paved with problems. It is man and the way the individual thinks and perceives it. Turn these around, come out of darkness and face the light and the love that can be felt for it will guide you through.

Those that have read the last few pages including many churches or places of worship may discount many things and say 'utter rubbish' or even 'the devil talking'. We understand that this may happen and it is okay. We are not commanding anyone or saying, "*This is your way or else*" or "*one rule or you do not succeed*". Every single one of you can open your heart to those around you. Is that talk of the devil or evil? Judge for yourselves - but we do say please progress so that learning becomes easier for you and those that you touch, those that you meet and for those that hold our their hand in friendship.

To many religions and those that think they have many gods, it does not really matter that 'God' is called this name or any other. What is important is that the individual can perceive and identify with and understand that there is the 'All'. That the very essence of life itself has been given in love and light in many forms and appearances for growth and for learning.

We must explain that we do not wish to say (and we may be repeating ourselves here) that you do not suddenly say, "What I have followed is utter rubbish, or what I have followed for years is wrong". Only you can do or say these things. Just open up your soul (spirit), your mind and your heart to other ways of thinking and do not 'box' yourself into any hard and fast particular 'religion' as it is only perceived and created by individuals. Many of them, so, so long ago. (PAUSE)

ME: This short poem then came through:

> *Be yourself, be true to yourself and your fellow man,*
> *do the very best that you can.*
> *Learn to live and to trust,*
> *be still, be one, and do not count just on us.*
>
> *We are all as important as one another,*
> *none more so that everyone of a family of each other.*
> *Love and light for every single thing,*
> *open up and let truth rain in.*

David, time is drawing close today and a small part of 'Lessons' has come your way. Much more to follow and to let flow and understand.

You be true and let the pen go on to explain more - you will see. Forever together, love, truth, peace, us and me.

ME: Thank you all, love and light I send to you all, forever.

FRIDAY 8th SEPTEMBER 1995

ME: I pray for the good in all things. The truth, the love, the light and for peace and harmony. Please let this pen flow in communication so that others may share and experience these things for the progress of mankind. Bless you all. Your son, David.

COMMUNICATION: We are here my son and the pen will flow and communication is and will be for all to share. Your 'will' will be done and continue as always so that others may seek and share as you say. We hope that what is given will be understood in many people's hearts and in their minds and that they can accept new ideas and feelings which is required for their growth and their progress.

We have spoken in our last time together of the beginning of 'Lessons'. Today this is continued by the middle phase or learning period which we have spoken about very briefly.

Many planets and civilisations like your own are embarking on this period of their existence, some for the first time and others that have got this far before (like yourselves). We hope and know that if mankind truly 'opens' itself from the youngest individual to the eldest and from the poorest to the richest, then you will achieve your inner goal and go on to the last but never ending phase of learning. (PAUSE)

'Lessons'. . . What is a lesson? From the earliest day at school and the child's apprehension of what is in store comes the fear and anguish of the unknown. As the child leaves it's mother's (or father's) outstretched hand and goes through the school gates, it is very frightened by the 'unknown'. Can you remember what your first real school day was like? (Maybe that will get you thinking).

Remember when the teacher guides the child and looks to the parent and says 'he/she will be okay, they are in fine hands'. Well, deep within yourself you are your own teacher. You are also your own guiding hand and have everything that will lead you to your goal, your peace, your truth and through your 'lesson'. Your lesson for life.

We could in a way also be called your teachers, helpers or even a classroom or learning centre to help each of you along the way. However it is down to the individual whether the lesson or page of the book is learnt, digested and taken on board.

We think that if you are reading this, then you are open minded enough to concentrate and proceed with the tasks in hand. Why pick up this book in the first place if it did not intrigue you or pose a question in your mind when you saw the front cover? Of course, many covers of books are misleading and people find that what is inside a book is nothing like they perceive it will be.

This is okay. Many may put the book back on the shelf while others may 'store' what they see, read and learn until they are ready to use or 'open up' to it. A bit like an exam in a way in what you learn, but in no way is this a compulsory test or one that if you do not accept right now, or understand right now, will it mean that you have failed.

Imagine a child or children that have come to this new school and they look around and see strangers and look so scared, apprehensive and confused. (Was that you?) - Well you are all the Creator's children and you are all (and will always be) going through the 'school' of life. You look around now and so much is about you that everything seems big and so hard to take in - the desks, the blackboard, the bells, the register, the food and new play times. So much to contend with and your moving along into your 'unknown', some may say a huge black hole.

Like all new things that have been (or are) difficult, some have had no help in their understanding and through no fault of their own, buried their head in the sand and have gone off the rails in life. Whose fault is that? People may say it is their own fault. "They did not want to learn or to achieve or to become 'something'." Are you sure?

Could they have had fears or no one to turn to? Did that child wish to become a loner or feel that he or she was a freak or outcast? All because someone has *judged* them *incorrectly* and has not given them a chance to express themselves or they did not have the guidance when it has been required or needed.

Maybe those that have judged, picked upon, bullied, cajoled, forced others or coerced them into being something which they are not will regret their actions and feelings towards others. Maybe the 'bully' or one that has neglected others will see in their heart their misgivings. They should think about that, because one day it may be too late for them to do so.

What can also be seen is that many have neglected their own 'inner' child, their own growth and understanding (which is understandable in your species) and been content with materialism in your lives. You have a job (or perhaps not), a home, a car, a family; you get up, you eat, you feed, you work and play and do all the things that you physically do.

Yet the biggest thing that is forgotten is the progress of your inner self and your heart and your mind. Too busy or too content? "Oh! I have achieved my goal!" or "I'm the best that I can become, I'm a director, manager, president or king".

As we have said before, is one better than the other? Maybe in what they earn or what 'power' they think they have. Yet inside and what they are made of is no different in any way. The 'tramp' can be more loving than any rich man. The road sweeper can be more helpful than the 'man' in the big fancy office controlling his 'millions'.

These are the things and feelings we want you to open up inside your hearts so that instead of looking in the classroom at the blackboard and the lesson today, look at what is structuring and is behind these things. The overall 'picture' and not just the page in the diary, the particular day in someone's life or any one part of your life as you so often perceive it.

Let us take you back again to the first day at school. You have met your new friends and your new teacher and gone through the first lesson. It is now your break, your first playtime in the new playground and this new 'space' has opened up before you. Some look through the door but stay inside and hold on to their coats or jackets while others expand and want to seek beyond their classroom boundary and are eager to learn new things. There are a few points we are trying to make here.

The first is that this 'playground' is what *you* perceive it to be and it can be infinite and everlasting or a few years as you know it. What is out there to be explored and learned? Does the playground have four sides and contain you like a box? What walls or barriers have you erected *yourself*? Go beyond the normal feelings and learn the things beyond your inside and everyday lives to seek fresh learning and new playing grounds of life.

Those that have stayed inside with their coats or jackets on need a helping hand to come out into the light and learn. Give a helping hand to those in need, (not just or only in a material, physical sense of course). There they stand wrapped up, covered up for many reasons or fears - "I'll be cold" or for fear of this extra unknown.

Help them take off this outer ring or layer of darkness and bring their hidden 'selves' into the light and warmth to this new truth and wisdom that *all* can feel. It is for sure that when they have truly opened up even in the smallest way and light has crept in, there will be a craving and yearning for more.

Do you remember your first school meal? Some will say "Yes! Unforgettable! Ugh! Horrible!" (We do not mean to simplify things but we have a sense of humour too of course,). How many of you said, "Please Sir, or Miss, may I have some more?" (An Oliver, perhaps?) Who and how many have been, or were refused? (PAUSE)

Some of you will find many things or information along your pathways of knowledge, truth and wisdom not to your liking or distasteful, or even upsetting to those that are close to you. We hope that much is digested and not spat out, but only you will know and time will tell.

The bottles of milk that you drank during your 'break' during your school days (only some will remember that!) gave you nourishment and strength to help you grow. To help your bones, your skeleton or infrastructure of your physical self.

We hope that the information that is sent from many walks of life including this one is another source of nourishment. As it flows within you it can give you a new strength, a new infrastructure which needs sustaining beyond your physical. This love and light is the true source of *all* and your life.

The end of the day is finally drawing near and the bell has sounded or the whistle blown. Time for you to leave the classroom and you can see love and warmth waiting at the gate again to take you home. You are asked "How did you get on? How many friends did you make? What was your teacher like? Did you have fun?"

As you gazed into your mother's(?) eyes and she held out her arms, you knew that the first day was over and a new phase had begun. It was not so bad and you even said, "I can't wait until tomorrow!"

Well, we hope you have understood and pushed aside any prejudices or trepidations because this learning has more than begun. Those that wish to learn can feel the love and immense light from where they have truly come from . . . and who and what is waiting for them when they get 'home'.

Life is like a school day in it's simplest form. Enter life like a lesson. Share in it, believe in it, love it and all the living things that are contained in and around you. The playground of truth and wisdom is there for you to all enjoy, to have fun and to grow, but is not and never will be a children's toy.

Be sincere in all your actions and believe in what you do is for progress for you and mankind and your fellow man. You all have so much to give of yourselves and of what is inside so open up and do not hide. Push aside all ill feelings and know that love will provide and sustain you on your journeys. (PAUSE)

Well, time again is drawing close and we will discuss and help again as much as we can. The final phase of your lessons (for some) is but a fragment of people's imaginations. We hope to explain a little more to help you know what lies in store. A beautiful, everlasting. . . Speak to you soon and our love is always here for you David and for you all. Goodbye, my son. Bless you all - Love, truth, peace, us and me.

ME: At this moment the feeling of love and peace around me was so beautiful and immense and I had to write. . .

Dear Father, you have given me the gift of life,
and how I wonder what has laid in store for me.
I feel your love and light surrounding me and filling my heart, my soul and mind,
and words they cannot say, just what I feel inside.
Your feelings cover my heart with light so beautiful that I cannot help but see . . . . .
Now only the truth and light that you have given me.
My very being aches with pain, yet a joy in the hope that more can feel and understand.
Your love so deep inside my very core, banishing hate, fear and sending love to end all wars.
Travel, time and life they do exists as one, to you my friends and family, the love and light I've now become!

Bless you all. Thank you.

MONDAY 18th SEPTEMBER 1995

ME: Dear Father, all of my family and friends and all those on every plane of existence I have known, do know and will know - draw close please, (as you always do). I am here to serve and share in your love and light. I am a mere speck of consciousness, yet special (as we all are) because we are made of love by the Creator, the Great Spirit. Please take my love and light with you.

I have missed you all in communication and this 'time' apart (due to my work) has made me feel so empty, yet you are always here. So strange these feelings. My pen is here today to write your love and wisdom and for your help so that this book can continue for others to learn too. Lessons part three now from the Two Sisters Star Group? My friends, my family, bless you all.

COMMUNICATION: Oh my son, we have missed you too. Even though as you say, we are close and are always with you. You have work to do (as we do too) so the gap can and sometimes cannot be helped.

Please never worry though because like you have said to many others, time is not important and things are done when they are meant to be done. It is so good to let the pen flow again and we let this work 'pair' in love and light. As it moves it will continue to say many things that you and many people will or will not understand until the time is right for them.

Let us begin with our final part of 'Lessons' - the end but no end. As we have said before, so much will await many of you who have opened your hearts in the right way.

Once those that have lived their lives in the right way and opened up within they will have used their sixth sense and also given up their dedications of 'want' for pure material gain. (Those who had nothing else in their hearts). They will then have gone on to show their true selves to others in peace and love and light. Their journey then has only just begun.

People may say "but I have given, I have shared, I have helped". Many do that but not in the right way. It is very easy for someone who has a lot of money for instance - with their millions, to say, "Here, I have donated". Donated what? Money? Yes, that has probably helped thousands of people in different ways, but he/she is missing the point. They have not given anything of themselves have they? What sacrifice did they make along the way? Time? Effort? (Physical or mental). Perhaps they could ask themselves, 'how much of a part did they play?'

Again and again we come back to 'opening' up in the proper way and believing and giving themselves in other ways apart from the materialism. There are so many workers of love and light that help others - a beautiful thing is a sacrifice to help another.

They too, need to open up. They have already made sacrifices but just need to work beyond the things that they do and understand themselves and their hearts. This will be easier for those that are, as we say, already helping others.

During their lives as this awareness and opening of their hearts is shown to them or understood, they will then 'become' so much more. On the Earth plane of existence you will then approach your physical death. Sometimes in such of a variety of ways, but ending the same. Confused? Don't be, we will explain.

We know that there are many of you that fear death. This is inbuilt like a safety valve that stops you (usually) from hurting yourselves. Some say it is an inbuilt 'fear' but it is only when that individual has gone astray (or has been led astray) and no one has come to aid them that they feel that they must depart and cannot live any more. So sad, . . . because all problems and all fears can be overcome with help and love from each other. Please all know that . . .

NO PROBLEM OR FEELINGS OF DESPAIR ARE TOO GREAT OR TOO INSURMOUNTABLE.

Before people state, "That is easy for them to say that. You are not living the pain, the anguish, the hate, or the racism". All we can say to reply to this is that we have experienced these things in a multitude of places and existences and in our own progress too.

Therefore we feel that we can help and pass on these words to help you with confidence. The Creator, your Great Spirit, your God has shown us the way a long, long time ago - before you even existed or were created. Move forward by turning 'within' for everything in the light and all around you will be revealed.

Let us carry on . . . You have feared death but you do not need to (ever) if you have lived in peace. Your physical self, your density keeps you where you are then it is no more. A shell and a home which had enabled you to feel, think, eat, sleep, work and do all the things that enabled you to grow on the Earth plane.

Then the time will come to pass or cross over into light and love - at the precise time that *you* have chosen. Those that have prolonged their earthly existence through transplants have chosen this. Whether you live or die, will always be what is meant to be. That is why those that cannot survive after these things are done come back home. No medical or scientific help that you possess can stop what is meant to happen if it is the inevitable. (PAUSE)

Many books and many teachers of many countries have explained 'cause and effect' so we feel that it is not necessary here. We are not your judges so we also shall not say whether these things that are done are right or wrong in any case. You will always have to come to learn and live with your own decisions and feelings in your heart.

Remember, love is the strongest force that exists. Love is infinite and everlasting and no time or distance can weaken or break true love. It is forever in the heart, never lost, never given away, never bargained for or weakened by others. True love - true light.

Your physical body ceases now and those around you and all who cared for you are close on all planes and on all dimensions. Separated, yet whole. Your physical world and those behind are devastated (but need not be), but also much rejoicing has begun. Your task has hopefully been completed and if you have lived in peace then your journey has begun again - for progress and continuance - an end but no end.

Some of you take time to 'adjust' and it is a while before you realise what has happened to you. You may feel lost or bewildered and do not understand when you see others close by. Everything is okay though as an understanding is there and the realisation hits home. This can be a shock or a wondrous thing depending on (we keep saying), how you have been and how you have lived the physical life.

As you, your 'self', your Soul, your Spirit accepts love that is all around you, the true immensity of it is indescribable. A rebirth in a true sense into everlasting peace and love and light - into wisdom, knowledge and progress - to reconnect in many different ways. It is unbelievable. So unbelievable that no matter what we say it will be hard to explain it to you. (N.B: There is no quick way to this love and light - and never can be! You will understand what we mean by this.)

Think of all the most beautiful things that you can ever imagine. A rainbow, a tear of sheer joy, your child you have just given birth to, your wedding (if it is true), your first kiss. Perhaps a butterfly in the sunshine on a breeze, the Seven Wonders of the Earth, your beautiful planet . . . roll everything into one and multiply it by infinity. This unbelievability that no one can truly comprehend is there. . . for you, if you truly want it and live in the right way.

You, the average person, can change so many things (and so many of you are) if you try and push aside all the bad things of life. Make those who *can* change things - those in power and in the position of responsibility, alter for good and peace. There is nothing, but nothing that *cannot* be achieved if you have the will to do so. Link together - become one. You have the chance to push 'religion' (those that 'box' and hem-in/resrict your very being) aside and to push 'hate' and 'want' aside *to bring love and peace into your hearts.* (PAUSE)

You, as an individual own nothing materialistic when you cross over. Do not place your 'all' in things that you can never take with you. This is hard we know. You think in many terms and ways of holding down possessions. We understand this and this has been your way for a long, long time.

When you die, your love continues as we have said. This is the only thing that is truly in place and handed down. When a mother loses her child and visits the 'grave', what does she care about? It is not the car, the house or the garden. Everything is in her heart - a true connection that can never part (as we have said), so do not worry about other things. The tears will flow and memories are within - you never die - you cannot ever. You are born of light and energy that cannot be split, crushed, dismantled or thrown away. You are together forever, in a fragment of time and space.

Do not ask if you are big or small, important or great as you all have your goal and life's task to achieve and they will be found within yourself. Believe in your love and your heart and that true life goes on in a different way. Could it be one hundred years, fifty years, tomorrow, today?

Turn to the light and you will all be saved. Turn to hate and darkness and you could be in pain for so long - released or maintained /held there - only you will know this when the time comes.

David, my son. Today is drawing close again and the pen is due to stop. So good that you have learned and can share this. Not all will understand. In time my son. We feel that there are so many things we could elaborate on but at this stage it is the 'simplistic' that counts. If someone can grasp what we are passing through you then when things are ready, more detail in further 'lessons' and 'works' will be appropriate for them and for *all*.

The lessons and the 'Pathway' of love and light is infinite. Pray for love and peace both by day and by night. Be one. Be still and share together to live your life's in light forever.

Goodbye my son, from all of us. Still to learn our name, we see. Keep trying, it is in your heart. More to follow in love and peace, and in truth and love from us all, always.

ME: Thank you from my heart. Love and light to you all forever. Your son and friend, David.

I sat still for a while longer and thought of those who had cut their lives short. (Before their time?) I also hoped that this information explaining that our love always remains and how it will always continue to be handed down will help many people who are, or have been grieving.

A personal friend and close family I know have been through so much in their lives. They have allowed me to share a special poem sent from their loved one who has crossed over. I hope it touches your heart as it did mine. . . it's simply called. . .

DANNY

A flower was born into this world,
that had already bloomed and its petals had dropped.
A longing for a life which I knew I'd left behind,
a longing for love, which I knew that I would find.

Crystal tears . . .
that fall from your cheeks.
I now catch and hold,
and kiss whilst you sleep.

A life in which I knew I had to go,
a story I told . . . hard to bear . . . hard to hold.
I feel the pain, in which I left to deal,
but yet there is not a moment, all of you feel.

Goodbye for now but not forever.
Believe me I am close,
however far or near,
on your paths of life . . . know that I am here.

I come with love, with compassion, with hope,
and grief is but a step, life unfortunately has to take.
So in your hand I will hold . . .
a flower that was born into this world.

And in my bloom . . . I give you all my love!

CHAPTER FOUR

'A NEW ERA'

FRIDAY 22nd SEPTEMBER 1995 10.00 a.m.

ME: I call to the Great White Spirit, our 'Creator'. Also to my dear family, friends, teachers, guides, helpers, gate keepers, ministers of healing and to all those I have known on every plane of existence . . . please hear me. You know and understand what I have gone through and felt this week and during this moment, I seek and pray for the progress you offer. Yet I know I must be patient, too.

There are so many different tracks and paths to take and I myself judge my own mistakes and in who I may have let down. Your strength is within me though and I touch it for the ability to go forward in peace and harmony and truth. I hope what I have said, thought and actioned has not detracted from our goal.

Please let the communication and pen flow . . . Chapter Four? You will always hold a special place in my heart (The Two Sisters' Star Group) and I hope to progress further; please can you help me? I love you all and always will. Please let this flow. . .

COMMUNICATION: David, David, David, why . . . why . . . why do you ever worry, my son? We understand and know of course of the way you feel. We have been there many, many times and so long ago and have never forgotten what it is like to progress (and we still are).

Time. All in time my son. We know of many others who are with you all the while, watching and listening to see how things are with you and around you. So never despair or never think that no one cares because you know love is infinite and love is nurturing and always, always forgiving for those with truth in their hearts and minds.

Your own progress you have chosen and as the time passes for you, you will understand this more and more. Follow your intuition (you should know) and the feeling within your heart. Others may follow and understand the decisions that you make and others may not. It does not matter because each will in whatever way is necessary for them when their own light is burning more brightly and their pathway is seen in front of them. Let things flow and if what you feel is for your progress, then follow it.

In time this will make much more sense, even if it does just a little for you right now. We know that one of the things you feel is frustration, this is okay. You know that what is learned is never handed on a plate. There would be no point for your progress or for yourself within. This applies to you all.

Love and be loved David. Everything is love so follow your feelings. Everything is there for you so just believe and believe in yourself even more and everything will fall in place and you *will* succeed.

Okay, let us carry on now - Chapter Four. It is hard to believe that we are nearly a third of the way through, yet it feels like only yesterday when we first began doesn't it? What do you think?

Chapter Four David, is about the 'New Era' that approaches for you and us and for millions of life forms in existence. We can begin to inform you of so many new things because the time is right for progress and yours too. We will never hold back on what is right for personal growth and important knowledge and wisdom (Two different things of course!). This new era and the new millennium is not very far away and so is the new beginning that we have discussed before.

Many, many centuries on your Earth plane have been considered as new eras. Right back to your present way of thinking and beyond. You look back on the time of the Stone Age, Bronze Age and move forward in time through steps of evolution with awe (in some respects). Yet how has mankind *really* progressed in the last two thousand years?

It may seem impressive to begin to explore or fly in the sky at the turn of the last century and now you have linked in space across different nations. What does this represent. . . growth? Searching? A completed goal? If you had joined together in peace and love and shared in experiences, each nation, each people would be far, far ahead of it's time as it is at present. (N.B: We are not condemning you, just stating what is fact).

We see it too, on the other worlds and planets. There is a place - not too dissimilar to yours that is about three hundred of your earth years in progress ahead of you. They have had many changes and many conflicts and much heartache to seek and to achieve what they believe is growth.

They are searching, they are looking and most of their species have begun to learn the right way by looking 'within' for real progress. Their light is getting brighter to join when all are ready and this will happen, make no mistake of that. We are able to reveal this planet's name to you as we have been 'allowed' to - in a sense - for this progress for all. The planet is not in your solar system and is called REAMILITUS. (Write as it sounds, David).

It's people, as we say, have advanced slightly ahead of yours but their technology does not have the ability to get to you or connect with you in any way. (It is not meant to, as yet). They have space travel within their own system but are not ready to go beyond that at its present speed of evolution. We will go into more of their particular existence when the time is right, (because it is very similar to yours) as we have said. The reason why we have mentioned them to you is this change - this new era that is approaching for you all.

It does not matter that life exists in all of the billions of systems and galaxies. Every single one is going through change and not just in the technological sense, but of the connection, this link to the Creator, your Great Spirit. What we believe is happening to mankind in particular is still unique though. Its new era is an example for others to follow. To be watched and to be seen to grow in purity and clarity of thought and of deed.

This new fragment of time and space is being created right now and the more light that is transcended from you and the people the faster it is coming together. As if being formed by building blocks of frequency and impulses of energy and life force.

It is of a new stability and of wondrous proportions, but when it is finished, no one will know. We think that as and when it is mankind's time and readiness to go there and to expand, it will touch 'in' and hit out like a million supernovas. Bursting out in all its brilliance - touching billions upon billions of 'souls' and 'beings' which are, (and will be) drawn to this peace and love like a magnet. Pulling them in to be touched by the Creator's love.

This may be hard for so many of you to comprehend and we understand this. It may be difficult to change the way of thinking of say, 'Darwin' and switch to this. So many even say, "There is nothing out there and we are all there is. You are born, you die, you turn to dust and that is it".

This is okay. One day perhaps to be open minded that is all we ask. Open to learn and to say, "Hey! That is interesting that point of view," while others will say "Please show me the proof and I will understand".

"Proof" we hear is a small word but with a big meaning. What is proof to one man is nothing more than a joke to another. Proof is all around and within every single one of you. Physical proof for those that need it, may or may not ever happen. Does that person need proof in them to move forward? What would an 'alien' spaceship in someone's back garden prove. . . that the individual has seen something? Does the photograph convince the world?

People will only believe in what they want to believe and this is evident in mankind's growth over the millennium. Wouldn't the mentality of many think they are being invaded and which authorities would think that they have the power to (and even think they could) hold or interrogate their new visitor(s)?

A hand of friendship has been given by so many of your people and it has been met with violence and the gun. We cannot let what is not meant to be revealed to you, until the time is ready - 'too much too soon', 'and do not run before you can walk' are very common phrases that you have used for such a long time. We would never want you to feel that we mistrust anyone or anything, but if mankind were in our position (and we wish you were, we really do) then maybe you would feel exactly the same, or even more so.

The 'eras' of time and of existence are for your learning process and your growth indeed. Yes, explore and branch out and increase awareness to all that is around. Do not restrict yourself to being on the ground or in the air or space, look beyond yourselves and the human race. Care and love every living thing - so do not hurt or kill what you see with a gun.

Pain, so much pain and darkness has spread. What a sacrifice you are giving up to hack down and to make dead. Look at all the living things that you have and are making extinct - love the things that you think, cannot think.

In this new era, you will truly see that there is a 'one', a peace and brilliant harmony and of no pain or want, greed or disdain - just love and light shining so, so bright. (PAUSE)

Think for a moment of your daily tasks - how do they affect others . . . and have you helped them along or through their day? Relieved any suffering or heartache or pain? Cut your finger and you will wince. So what does the insect or the animal or tree feel when it has been cut down and almost left without a trace? You do not realise what you are doing to *yourselves* and you must feel this in your hearts. (PAUSE)

We have briefly touched on the new era that awaits for mankind and every living race. Please move forward in strength and conviction. Be guided by what is within and around you by opening your hearts (sorry if you feel that we keep 'going on') and radiating the light to others. You will then give more of yourself and so much more to assist and create what is meant to be. For you and also for me.

A NEW ERA

An era of Love and immense magical beauty,
branching out and touching 'all', for eternity.
Link together and stretch out a cord of love and light,
you can do this for yourself, mankind and all and every life.
It is easy just proceed, be one, still and rest,
this is most important, Love for everything . . . a true test?

David, today draws to a close my son. We feel your love in your heart and you know we are linked and will never part. Be true in everything you say and do - do not feel lonely cold or blue. Peace within and the light will shine forever and ever for all 'time'.

Be true, love from us to you. Peace, truth, love and harmony will always be.

ME: I give my hand of friendship to you all, bless you for connecting to me. I will understand and know that you are always with me. My love and light to you all. My guides and teachers and the Great Spirit, my family and thee. . . Truth and love, blessed be.

MONDAY 25th SEPTEMBER 1995 9.50 a.m.

ME: Hi again from me and my heart! I know that we are all one, never able to part. Please be with me as always in truth and love. Guided as always by the Great Spirit, the Creator above.

To those that have insight and communication through me, let the pen flow with your peace and harmony. I am here for the future and for now, let this pen flow - please - you know how. My love, my heart lies open in the light for you to draw close just as you are right now, giving us part of your life. . . N.B: (I could then feel such energy around me - the candle flame was flickering, weaving and dancing - it was wonderful.) Then. . .

COMMUNICATION: Hi, David my son! See how the senses click in and communication begins. Peace and love remains true and is all around, waiting for each and every individual, in their hearts it is found. Destiny and life is in each of their hands in waiting and learning, each country, each nation and each land.

Time is near to start afresh and to be free from ill and hate and the entangled mesh. What is the darkness and the things that drag you down, you each will cast aside and in light and love be 'found'. You will all realise that this is the true consistency of you, me and the pure frequency. This is all and

71

all is this. Be one, be still, to learn and be free and you will never miss.

The new era continues for all those in truth and it will never labour or diverse in a wrong direction. (It cannot, no matter what is said and done by anyone). This is the Creator's wish and it can only be fulfilled.

As the new era approaches and all those that are ready to join together and become 'one', there will be immense heat and light that is given off. You could say another 'big bang' as some on the Earth plane have described it, (your beginning of 'time', that is). Things will not be the same as before though.

Millions of your Earth years and evolution has been completed. The pulling together of infinite life and love - the harnessing of star systems, planets created and destroyed, suns born and moons split to harmonise and equalise everything around. All this was completed when it was required to be.

This new era is so, so different. So different from that which has all gone before. Yes, a 'bang' but not in your earthly sense of destruction, explosion or devastation. This is rebirth, of light manifested and ejected in all directions and strength inconceivable because it is infinite. It will enter and touch every single galaxy, solar system and encase every star, planet and beyond and. . . beyond. As this happens there will be a drawing together to this new place and existence that even we can only *begin* to imagine.

Your planet, along with so many others will not exist as it does at present. Those that will be required will ascend both spiritually - your spirit, your soul *and* your physical presence will enter the light with new tasks to do. Do not be left in darkness by continuing to be the way you are. Change to love, peace and truth as only joy and true, true love will shine through to enable you to become what you are meant to be so follow your heart into your destiny.

Mankind as such will be a very important part of the jigsaw because of the way you have been created and your ability to be so diverse in feelings and communication. What lies beyond is a mammoth task but it can be done. All the species and life forms that will come together will have their own tasks to do too, but it is the linking together that is and will be so important.

What is going to be achieved will last for eternity. An expression of the Creator and its plan of evolvement for each of us and each 'speck' of consciousness no matter how diverse and how unfamiliar it is to anyone or anything else. (PAUSE)

The Great Spirit, the Creator has not as we have indicated suddenly decided this yesterday or the day before. The progress has, as we said earlier, been 'monumentous' in preparation and dedication to every living thing in every dimension. Sometimes our minds have trouble to conceive this immensity and complex existence.

We would like to describe what we know of the Creator but at this present time it is not right for us to do. Not that we are holding back, but we feel that later on it would be more appropriate. Another species said it 'blew their minds', not literally of course, but the fascination of what was described and learned.

The connection that you will give to others and other species and life forms will be natural to all those that are there to do so. There will be assistance and guidance of course where it is needed or requested, but all along you have everything within you. A connection to your higher self and to the Creator. So it is 'within' that everything lies ahead and after this rebirth it will be able to be achieved.

You will all grow and continue to grow forever together. Can you imagine what that will be like for you all that link together! All the interconnections, knowledge and wisdom, love and harmony, it will be beyond comprehension and beauty, it truly will.

These same messages and teachings are continuing all over and those life forms and species everywhere are preparing too. Some faster and some slower than you are. Pace will pick up and proof everywhere will be seen of this.

For you on the Earth plane, many 'old' souls being reborn (physically) will carry the last few over - those that wish to be and those that have been slightly diversed and *have* tried to get back on the right pathway in their lives too. They are some unique 'teachers' and have gifts (as you all do) that will help this 'cross over', this Ascension when the time is right.

People will grow with them and learn from them to then teach others so that their task is continued and spread in all directions and further afield. (As has and is being done at the present time.) Many of you will totally change your lives and personalities in different ways. Not to be alienated from your families and those you love but in a way you are yourself. The way you act inside and tune in to your true 'higher self'.

This is a gradual process for some, but others, like a bolt of lightning encasing your world and the way you live your life. Your eyes will be truly opened and you will see life in a new perspective, and thus, feel so very differently. It will captivate you and tug your heart. Tears will flow and your emotional relief and joy will enter your heart because you will be 'different' on a soul level.

Understanding and inner growth will flow from this and acceptance too. Never ever fear this because it will happen and affect all lives at some point and it is something so precious, so beautiful and only *you* will know that this has happened to you. No one will ever judge you because they cannot. You will know in your heart and your mind and in your soul that what is about to take place is immense love everlasting.

Touch it and be touched and you can never look back, only forward. Those you love and those around you will follow when they are ready to and not before. One thing is for sure and that is if they have opened up, they will never be far behind and (they will never be lost) - one together - *always*.

Many people reading this book and this chapter on the new era will be saying "Hey, okay. . . When?" We understand this. Oh, it would be so easy for us to say the exact time and date, the day, the month and the year. We do know when it will be, but even though we are here to help you and know so many things, we feel that there would be very little achieved in telling you.

The Creator does things at 'its' own pace and in any case, there is a universal time for it (as we have said) so it does not cover just one planet or species. It will affect all, when everything is in place to do so.

Natural progress, natural laws for one and for all. No privileges, no acceptances, no pardons, no misgivings - each to their own and each fulfilling themselves and their destinies. It is like those teachers we described. They do not ask whether they are big or small. . . (this line has been given before and David, you know it). . . because even the grain of sand on the beach is important. It makes one 'whole'.

Likewise, the child and the test, the teenager and the exam, the surgeon and the heart operation. If you do not try or do not do, you cannot learn. If the answer was always in front of you, you would never use your mind, your very being and your Soul. Mankind would have never progressed even to where they are now!

You grow because you desire it and you learn from it. You try and sometimes you fail but you try so you have learned. You will not always get things right but as long as you do or have tried to do the right things, then you can and will progress. What were the consequences of your actions to others and everything around you? Look inwards and outwards for the answers, always.

Time is again drawing near my son and this chapter was quite short - enough said on this for now. Chapter Five next. . . well, do we grin or do we tell. There is a joy and feeling in the growth we see, an expansion. So we want to continue with this and not the new era as this new connection and expansion will describe more of the link between everything. You will see as it will all become clearer.

David, love and live and live in love. Feel and become part of everything that you already are. Till next time my son in love, truth, peace and me.

ME: Thank you to you all from my heart. I will know, do know and always know you are with me. Love from me to thee, always. David.

CHAPTER FIVE

'EXPANSION'

FRIDAY 29th SEPTEMBER 1995 11.20 a.m.

ME: In peace, love, truth, light and harmony I welcome those that draw close, who are within and around me and for my progress and understanding. I hope and pray through the Great Spirit that today the pen will flow in communication - Chapter Five, EXPANSION. I look forward to this as always for my own growth and so that the world may share and continue their pathway and destiny into light. Bless you all.

COMMUNICATION: David, what have you done to become what you are? To open up, to be still? Yes there have been many changes in your life and in your heart and some things that have shocked you while others have passed by without notice.

A 'release' from within yourself that is touching (and has touched) others so that they can progress too. This in a way is an 'expansion', a link. You see, all those that are connecting to the light sometimes do not know they are even doing it, because it is a natural thing from within and from around them.

Last time, we explained how the branching out, the new era would begin. Today is about the expansion that will take you and the people there and beyond. Not a backward step, but a continuance, a link to eternity and everlasting light and love.

Even the most loving person and those of deep religious standing and beliefs do not, or cannot sometimes feel this special link that allows them to touch and to teach others. It is like an inbuilt timing device or the creation of a feeling that is within your very being and in the heart.

Every single person has it, but it often lies buried so deep within the darkness and problems of your everyday lives that it is a very difficult task for it to shine and to touch others so that it can grow and develop. Know that this link, this light that expands, is so beautiful.

Although we have touched on energy 'flows' before, this is such a wonderful thing that we wanted to 'EXPAND' on this too. So perhaps even if just one other person was to understand and open up their 'self', then progress would have been made. (PAUSE)

There is a universal life force that is in every single being. Everything that is life from the flower, the insect, you, us, the Earth, the planets, the moons, the stars, the millions of species in every galaxy and solar system. A life force of light, energy and love. You cannot touch it, you cannot make it, you cannot break it, yet you can expand it. Weird that, isn't it?

Growth and expansion, everlasting and universal. Imagine if you possibly can, a matrix of connections. For example, a grid of computer components, a spider's web that seems to get larger and larger in the glistening early morning sunshine or a maze that you have entered with so many turnings, but which way do you go? Onwards, inwards, sideways, backwards? If you are lost you would/could go on forever if the doorway out could not be found?

Well the link is like all of these. It can be infinite, if you want it to be. (The individual, that is.) Personal growth is everlasting no matter what and who you are and nothing ever dies but is reborn. (That statement may cause a few disruptions we are sure.) So the link that you have 'within', and the connection between you all is always there and it can grow or remain lost, just like you're in a maze. The maze of worry, disease and decay - not finding the true you or your true pathway.

Personal expansion is not about these negative things, but of growing and connecting with others by being reborn into a new way of thinking and of 'being'. It affects you all and everything as we have said and what you do today is your tomorrow and your future is today. Make it what you will.

The light and love that is being created by you all is linking all 'over' in your time, our time, all *time*. Yet you do not realise that there is so much more that is waiting for you to achieve and what you are destined to do. We are all linked and so it has always been for millions of years.

Many watch and wait. Some debate and hold their heads in their hands when confusion and destruction reigns in many of your countries but we cannot and would not interfere (even if we or others could).

What we do see in certain pockets over your globe is the light and love spiralling like a network of lines which are quite beautiful, we can assure you. They form a grid around the planet when connected but because they are still so far apart, darkness is so easily sucked through and out of the gaps.

In time as the light and link expands, the gaps will become smaller and the people and their very beings will shine so brightly that it will cover the Earth like a casing. A hardened shell so strong that will enable the main cord to be expelled from its centre.

All that have attained or are on their destinies and correct pathways will link and be in this cord of beautiful light as it bursts upwards into and beyond your 'SPACE' and dimensions to go to your new home of everlasting peace.

As this time approaches and is about to happen, many other worlds at the same time will be going through the same event and the same destiny. So expansion is connected way, way, way further than you can possibly imagine or comprehend.

If you can try to picture this please do so. A small centre circle of light in your mind, all darkness around it. Suddenly, from every direction and every corner of your mind comes a beam, a cord of light to this centre spot, each at the same time. Your mind is then lit with a brilliant light. Not blinding but is 'all light' - no darkness anywhere because the light has expanded beyond your mind and continues forever, everything connected.

No time and space can hold it back, it is everlasting. No words can really describe this and we doubt they will ever be able to. When *we* are experiencing it, we too will only ever know at that moment. (Such love, so much love we will have ever known.)

The cords of light we spoke about, coming from all directions, will hold so much. Hope, truth, light, peace, togetherness, beauty, love, harmony, trust, goodwill, wisdom, knowledge and these will carry every experience from everything and its source. From its beginning, from its early birth and 'flux' of energy to what you and they (all) are today and *on that* day.

What combination, to be all those things and what they have and will become. There will never again be a need to worry or hate, despair or to destroy. THINGS LIKE THAT WILL BE LEFT BEHIND WITH THOSE THAT HAVE NOT GROWN OR HAD THE DESIRE TO.

The Creator will, we are sure, feel like its children are truly home and this 'learning period' that we have all undergone (so far) will be over. To embrace and be embraced. The magnitude of this is truly remarkable and as we think about what you write David, we still sit in 'awe' of what the Creator is putting together in pureness and its light. (PAUSE)

We would like you to come once again on a short journey with us. We have heard you ask this a few times recently and we wish it too. Be still David and just enjoy. Your heart will be opened and you can describe this experience too. Do not ever be afraid. We know you are not but are sometimes apprehensive which we understand. Relax my son. You will find out more of what you want to know . . .

ME: At this point, 'time' and me just seemed to drift then . . .

COMMUNICATION: Describe your experience David, and what you feel - it is part of the link and expansion we described. It will flow and because it is of 'this' that it fits in with what we are trying to say to you all.

We are with you as always my son, in light, love and in truth. Be one as always in love, peace, truth and us. Goodbye and love to you all.

ME: What I felt and experienced was wonderful. Such peace and feeling of togetherness - not separated by time or distance or the fact that we were different. It was as if I was 'one', a part of 'everything' for a short while. I am not really sure how long this lasted for. Five/ten minutes or more?

I had suddenly felt I was being drawn upwards with such a beautiful feeling of summer, light and heat. I was walking through a golden field, butterflies were around me. It was as if it was stating that I was in natural surroundings. After a moment I sensed a drawing close of something quite large and a soft light descended upon me and fast movement followed.

I knew a journey of a kind had begun and it was quite weird. It was as if I was looking out of a window into space and the stars. Jupiter went by and it seemed as if there was a pause to reflect on the beauty of what was seen. . . before passing by the Sun.

People may say, "In what way and how did you perceive the things you saw?" The Sun just seemed like a huge yellow/orange mass for instance. I have seen films on TV of the Sun and the emittance of its surface but what I saw probably meant we were not right next to it. (It was as if a 'fly-by' in a sense.) After a while the movement stopped and my perception of everything confused me. My vision for instance. Was I under or outside of a building of some kind?

I looked out into space and I saw what looked like two planets. A voice said, "That is ANDOREAS and that one is ELIXUIR," It was revealed that Andoreas was a moon but that Elixuir, which was so beautiful, was special. It gave them life - 'from this we were born' - was the message. (It was a brilliant white sphere, like a white marble against a black velvet background. Picture Twelve: 'VIEW FROM A CRAFT' page 79).

PICTURE TWELVE: VIEW FROM A CRAFT

A funny thing whilst here was that I did not seem to walk anywhere, as if my vision 'carried' me. I went down a corridor. It was in this that the specks of light (one of their 'bodies'/forms of existence) were down along either side. I could feel them as I went by. Just as if you could hold out a hand and touch them . . . yet they seemed to brush by me!

At the end of the corridor a multiple coloured sphere with edges, stood on a sort of 'holder' (image of holder was blurred by the light). All above it were floods of colour. Purples and blues and all around its base were yellows, reds and greens. I asked in my mind, 'what is that for?' An answer came, "It is part of what sustains and nourishes us." (Picture Thirteen: 'THE ORB' page 81.)

A second or two(?) passed and in front of me was only what I can describe as a control panel. However, my vision could only see the part where my hand suddenly appeared to be. I placed it over it and I could see flashes of star systems - as if on a screen. A thin hand was above mine which then took my hand away and it (the flashes of systems) stopped. A voice said, "How appropriate." As if amazed. "This is *your* system." This apparatus or machine seemed to contain maps of all the solar systems. I did not ask though. It was as if I just knew (Picture Forteen: 'INSIDE' -(A) and (B) page 82.)

I moved away and everything was blurred again. After this I could sense a closing in around me with such a feeling of peace, love and friendship. Five of them drew close and I hugged each of them. One of which I could tell (or knew) was a female. I remember gazing at a small hole on the side of her head - realising that it must be their ears/an ear hole. I then gazed into their eyes. They were deep, deep black, yet not in the least 'dark' - how strange!

At this point I knew it was time for me to go and I began drifting up and up and up as if in a 'light vacuum'. I looked down trying to see at speed. A scene of crystal blue and white lines (?) were getting smaller (as if on a building, a city, or complex or even a craft of some sort). Actually, this almost resembled the pupil of an eye. (Picture Fourteen: 'INSIDE" -(C) page 82.) Another few seconds passed (sorry, but this is what it seemed like) and I felt an intense pressure all around my head as I became aware of myself again sitting in my room.

After all of this, I wonder how do you think I felt? Strange? It is all so hard to describe really. To see wonderful things and experience it with certain senses, hearing, seeing, touching (no taste or smell of anything though) and of course, with my heart.

Yes, we are ALL part of each other and of everything. This has expanded my thinking yet again - another link indeed. In the images I have drawn I hope that they can portray just a little of this 'experience'. They are truly things that I will remember forever and a day.

(NB) Thank you for this experience. Bless you all.

PICTURE THIRTEEN: 'THE ORB'

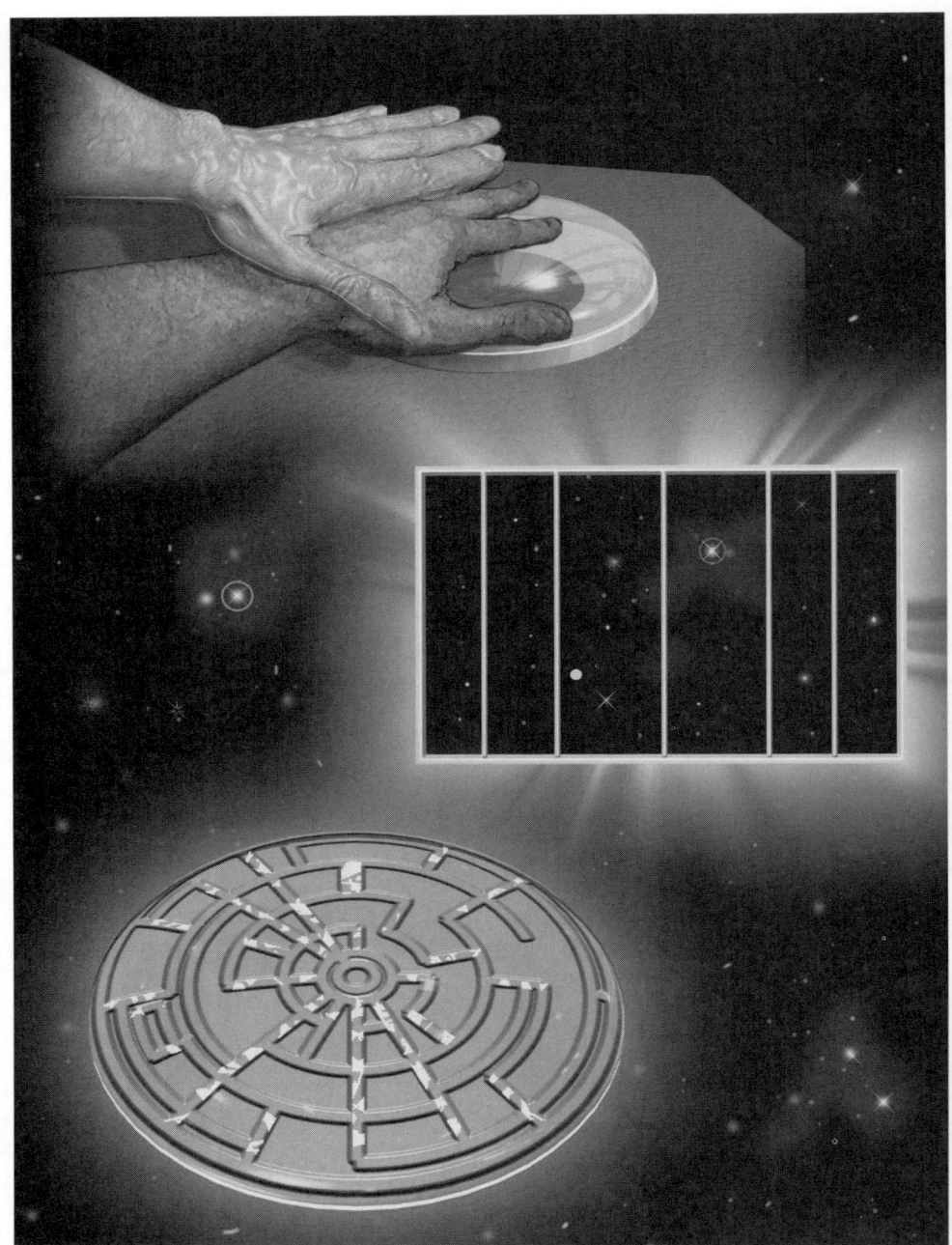

PICTURE FOURTEEN: INSIDE - A, B + C

CHAPTER SIX

'THE WONDER'

TUESDAY 3rd OCTOBER 1995 9.15 a.m.

ME: Heavenly Father, the Great Spirit, our Creator, all of my family and friends, teachers and guides I know you are all within and around me. You know so well of that what concerns and troubles me and of my hopes, desires and wishes. But I know that in faith, love and light we are one and that is all I need to continue to achieve what is meant to be - my destiny.

My friends and family from the Two Sisters' Star Group please let the pen flow and communication continue so that we can all learn and live in light and truth. Will 'EXPANSION' continue today or will a new chapter begin? (Even though the last one would then be so short?) Please let us begin and feel your love and guidance. Thank you. Your son David.

COMMUNICATION: Bask in the light, the wonderful light and warmth my son. It is there, here and everywhere for you and you all. When troubles and worries or your concerns seem too much, just learn to turn within as always and turn to faith and trust. Never worry, never despair, your worries and cares are always listened to, but sometimes, as you know, they must take their proper 'course' - of course. Cause and effect and natural laws as always but you can each alter your destinies in the one and only correct way.

Your love and light shines through and nothing will ever stop it. So just take each day, each step and you will succeed as we have told you many times before. Have faith, strong faith and your trust will see you through. Pass this on to those around you and give them the strength, your strength, to overcome the trials and tribulations that you all go through. It will carry you and sustain you. Believe us, we know, as we have been through it so long ago.

Let us pause and reflect and look upon what we have gone through so far together. Understanding, to live and love, connections, lessons, expansion, a new era, love and light, nourishment and energy and 'fluxes'. How much more? So much more David and you will see.

Let your pen flow as you have asked and so it shall be and you will read and write and you will 'see' as all will in their own time. We hear you ask, "what next?" and ponder, well here it is. . . THE WONDER. Does this makes you think?

Well this is a new chapter and you were right in that the last was so very short. No more needs to be said just yet on 'Expansion'. Here today, we have said and called this the 'Wonder' because of two things. These are your people and the many other species inner 'SEARCH', and also for that which is the Creator.

It is a 'wonder' because of what little so many have as a perception of it. A God, a Great Spirit or whatever name or terminology you or anyone has called the Creator throughout the millennium. Today is about the search in each and every living thing's heart and minds.

Let us go right back now to your own days in this lifetime when you were a small boy. Many questions asked with eyes opened wide, to search and *wonder* at everything and we see that many still do. This brings a smile to us, a joy because it means that you (the person) is not just content to accept everything that 'is'.

Many questions are posed and not many answers are given by the people or found in the places in which to answer them, half the time. This is because it is looked for in the wrong *place*, in the first place! This is not a true mistake but a 'learning' process for that person or because the people giving the advice are misguided or incorrect themselves.

Thus, it makes someone confused, bewildered and lost. To then search even longer and harder when many things are and always have been so simple. Such complexity, yet so simplistic. You are truly fascinating to watch and to comprehend and as we have said before you are all 'unique'.

Many years ago you looked from a window and said Why? and How? Why am I here? What reason and what purpose will I serve? By now and even as you write you know these answers of course. Yet now they pose even more questions but it will be easier for you to know and to understand.

As you looked from the window and gazed out upon the passing world and all its fast things you had your feelings 'within' of doubt and fear. Your answers never came to you - or did they? You did feel a pull of the heart David didn't you. Yet you never quite grasped it at the time? So young, yet so old as many of you on the Earth plane really are.

You have all been through so much and so much 'time' and experiences have passed through and around you. It is so unbelievable, yet so true. SO FAR YOU HAVE COME THROUGH IT. Even though you do not/have not/or those that cannot, realise this at this present time. So many life times and so much pain, hurt and also joy has flowered yet you still feel lost sometimes but not forever.

Look forward and beyond and at today's beauty, light and love amongst the darkness and hate. As the sun rises and sets, as the small chick takes it's first flight, as the baby first cries and sheds it's first tear, your first kiss and your first hug of the one you have loved for so long and waited for. So much you can wonder at and perceive as true light, yet can be many times taken for granted even by those most 'true'.

We ask you to look for the hand that guides you (not always literally) and the hand of friendship and trust. Believe in it, nurture it and take it for what it is and for where it can lead you. Even though it may take you into the unknown. You <u>will</u> know in your hearts when it arrives, as it will embrace you. This is a wonder in itself. Acceptance and understanding the peace and the tranquillity that all should have and all should experience for themselves. From the oldest of mankind to the smallest child and each and every living thing. One day you will truly see.

Let us trace our steps for a moment and continue your search to be fulfilled or to feel the emptiness and sometimes the pain in your hearts. The search has been so hard and so long you think it will never end for that what is in your heart and in your heart's desire. Not material things, but for that which is so very much more important. This emptiness, sometimes feeling like a gulf so wide, so far and the road never ending, one more corner, one more obstacle. "Why? Why? Why? Will the road never end and my search be over? I look and I stare into the sky, I glare for an answer and still I wait and my tears flow. They roll down my cheek and I taste them on my lips. Tears of love (which love, what love?) that I do not know yet." Sometimes bitter, sometimes sweet, but a guarantee one day that you *will* meet.

Out of the window and into the light, this will become easier as the passing of each day and long nights. Many people will think of two loves, one on the Earth plane and it's many different forms and one in their beliefs, their 'wonder', their 'God'.

Love is always the same love. It cannot be divided or split into fractions, even though sometimes you unconsciously do. It may seem that you love someone more than another, say a brother or sister. On the outside this may appear so, but within - you cannot and do not. One day all will understand this. You are one, connected by everything and the Creator.

When you wonder of love, it is a magical thing. Such nervousness, apprehension, worry and concern that he/she may not feel the same way. Will your love be returned? Your stomach churns over and over and you cannot eat or sleep for the fear of the *unknown* and of what or will be the outcome. What will they think? What do they think of me? Shall I ask or will I see? After a while and the time passes you find out as you understand from yourself or from a friend. What will the future hold for us? Will we last? Will we turn to lust or hate?

Look at this from another viewpoint, another angle. Those that have turned within themselves and seen the light and beauty around them, know *all* the answers to love and its many comparables. On the surface as you face the testing time and you have asked the 'why', the Creator does not turn away or cast you aside - never - ever, but it is this feeling that you have been that *must* be eroded away.

In your God, your Great Spirit, the Creator, lies all the answers. So when you gaze out of the window (out from your heart) and the pain is so much to bear, look and turn within and you will find the answers to all your cares. In an instant or over time? Will your experience behold or turn out to be a crime?

Living a true love will bring peace and harmony to your individual world and close family and will expand to others close and also far around you. Gaze out of your window from your heart and you will never be lonely, cold or apart from those you love and the true love that it *is* and always will be. (PAUSE)

On a slightly different track now let us comprehend what so many species and civilisations have 'felt' over so long a 'time'. Back to one of your 'eras' when the first apeman walked or crawled (?) the Earth plane. Was he intelligent or docile as many today even think? He gazed upon the stars, the sun and the moon and knew them as 'Gods' as have many throughout your time. The sun was a God because it shone and brought warmth, light and growth. The moon brought light to the night to light the way and the stars were 'God's' children playing in the night sky.

Funny, or such a serious thought to those at the time? What we wish to say is that their beliefs in the 'wonder' were no less strange than that of many years or 'eras' that followed because of the strength in *belief* of those that lived at that time. Or were they wrong?

Looking at your religions over the last few thousands of years and the turmoil and also the peace (sometimes) it has brought is no different because they all *believed* for one reason or another.

Was it the leader, the King, the president or an event of spectacular natural law that created the way they felt? They have all wondered and looked above and said 'My God' or 'Our God' and many of the religions still do. So many different names yet every single one is the same. (That will cause a few ripples we think!)

It is the WONDER of it all and we see so many pray in faith so strong but have their beliefs in one hand and in the other, a gun. You cannot preach and become 'one' one day and kill and fight the next (or as we have seen sometimes, the SAME DAY). Those that do this will of course learn but it may be too late as we have said before.

Part of this 'wonder' is now over today but it will continue again when the flow will resume. We hope to let you know a little more about the *course* of you and your search, your 'wonder' that the Creator has instilled in you and in...'all'.

'WONDER'

When the snow falls and covers your home,
When the sun shines and melts it all away,
When the rain falls and wets your hair and your face,
When the wind blows and dries you and leaves without a trace.
When the rainbow forms across the valley,
When the lightening cracks the tree,
When the rivers give life to the land,
When the light brings a new dawn to wake up your mind.
When the night draws close and you shut the door,
Think of all the 'wonders' that be,
What has given you life and sustained 'me'.
Such a mystery or is it really?
Turn within, for true love is ALWAYS with thee.

Open your heart, your window to the true you,
So one day when you can accept,
You are born again. . . to face no more tests.

Speak to you soon my son, love to you all from us. Peace, truth, love and light, bless you all both day and night. Goodbye my son.

ME: I felt so at peace. Such love and warmth. Thank you to all those around and to those above. Thank you Great Spirit, to all my teachers, family and friends, till the pen flows once again.

THURSDAY 5th OCTOBER 1995 9.15 a.m.

ME: As the light shines within and around me I can feel all of your love, from 'in' and below and above. I pray for this 'Earth plane' to be 'still' and to learn to love all things, for within love there is peace and truth.

Please let this pen flow in communication as has been said to me. Let us (if we can) know more about the 'wonder', the splendour - our 'Creator'. Bless you all, the Great Spirit, my family and friends, teachers and guides. My life is your life and I follow the light everlasting in my heart's centre.

Please let us grow; please let us know, so this 'light' here can shine brighter and brighter.

COMMUNICATION: Hi David. We are here to speak and to let you know as always.

Good morning or is it good night, wherever 'you' are as you read this. Know that the light shines wherever you are and always so brightly that if you want to see, you can. Whether you feel so far away from anyone or anything you are never, ever, ever alone.

You can be in the deepest cave or on top of the tallest mountain, or feel lost in the wide and deep oceans or crawling in the sand. 'There' you will find that you are home in the light and at peace, no matter what 'pain' or struggle or hardship you are or appear to be going through. A real fear or a false one? You could be so scared and fear you may 'cease', but you would never need to worry or concern yourself in that way if you have lived your life in truth. (This is something we will discuss at a later date when it is more appropriate).

Yes, the 'wonder', the Creator, is all around wherever you go as we have just said and this is part of today's information for *you* or those that have just begun to read and learn of what we have to say. (Not all will learn or accept this we know of course - yet).

How then can 'God' or whatever name has been given by all and every species be 'here, there and everywhere'? (It could of course just blow your mind even at that statement alone). Firstly, how is it even conceivable to think that:

a) There is a 'God'?
b) If there is, how can 'he', 'she', 'it', be everywhere?
c) If there is, why does it never intervene when there is so much pain?

Well, since the beginning of 'time' (mmm. . . we could teach you so much on that alone but suffice to say. . .) when the 'Creator' made the first steps to let energy 'flow' out of itself, every living thing in every galaxy that has grown and then had the ability to 'think', has tried to perceive its existence. It's very being and how it was manifested.

Yes, we know that 'mankind' has developed and grown and your scientists and professors over the centuries have worked out certain things of this growth, but not about the very *beginning,* and where the 'all' was from. In every conceivable and inconceivable shape or size, in every cell or molecular structure, matter/anti-matter was and is in effect, 'born of energy' and energy is love. Immense love for sure. (PAUSE)

There has never been a species anywhere in existence that has *totally* thought that nothing like a 'God' has ever existed.

Every single 'one' - (there are *millions*) - and every single 'thing' as we have said, that lives and/or 'thinks' is connected to the one source, the 'Creator'. Therefore because this is so, there is an inbuilt feeling of togetherness, oneness of a 'whole' if you like, that can never be erased.

People and mankind have, due to their learning process, often denied it (within themselves) of course and this is part of the darkness and of your uniqueness that gives you individualities and choices. The Creator has never ever on your world forced living things to 'believe' or accept because at some point in any of your lives (and your individual *lifes*), you will. Probably there will be (and is) so much scorn and scepticism by some who read this and this is okay. We understand your views but you *will* change, we guarantee it.

If there was no conflict of opinions and no differences then you would all have progressed far beyond your present state (this time around) but as we can all see by not opening your eyes, ears and heart this is not the case the world over. (Which gives rise to one of the main reasons why this book is being collated together!).

We know that many of you that look around see the beauty that has been born on your planet. The same feeling many times over and over again on so many others across the galaxies and cosmos and it is within this that the awe of things is thought of and the wonder of it too.

How can all of these places and all of these dimensions be born into existence? How could anything construct so much? Let us look at certain things for a moment.

Let us first acknowledge that the Creator knows all and is everywhere. As this is the case, there is unquantified power and energy of that which even we could not begin to describe. The Creator could extinguish all life and every living thing in an *instant* in the same way that all was born. When this is perceived then it becomes easier to understand that of what the Creator 'is' and always has been and always shall be.

The Creator is love of course and this is why 'he' has never intervened. (More of that in a moment for we will explain ourselves). This inconceivable energy, infinite, everlasting and ever growing, emitted part of itself billions and billions of years ago in millions of directions at millions of different speeds. Each with it's own purpose and destiny and eventually to return home to be 'one' again. We have often asked how this must have 'felt' because 'it' surely did. How does a mother feel when she gave birth to her *wanted* child? Immense love that you cannot describe and this is why this is so hard to imagine and quantify.

Perhaps no 'one' could comprehend the feeling as the Creator let it's energy flow from itself. It must have been the most beautiful sight. Yet just as when a child grows and experiences the *world* with the feelings along the way of the love, hate, friendship, pain, joy etc., and even though the Creator knew (and knows) the end result of everything - the release must have 'ached'. This is why we will all be returning to the one true light and to return to our true home.

Billions of years have passed for us all from this beginning of 'time' and things are and will be connecting and coming together because it is in all of our destinies. Some may feel that they cannot wait and of course there is no quick way to this peace (as we have said before).

What must be done is hard work by all of you and in very different ways because of your individuality and learning stages. What is right for one will not be for another and vice versa. What one individual does is not the *only* correct way so do not let anyone chastise or say, "Hey, you must do this or else. You must pray this way or not at all, or you must help others there or here".

You and you alone from your heart lays the answer and you must follow it. Everything in life is okay is it not, if it does not hurt or inflict pain on any other living thing. It is this togetherness and helping each other that will speed things along and create the 'light' required for achieving the goal - the 'ascension' of mankind to it's real home in love and light.

The time for pain and anguish is *over*. Please, it must stop *now* for each of your sakes and for all those on the verge of extinction, your animals and your insects. How can/could you stand by and watch other living things perish? They are part of your existence and everlasting history and your future too.

This is the advice and we hope you listen, but we will not condemn or judge you and we hope that we have not exerted more pressure on you in these words. If we have then perhaps it was meant to be. To possibly open up one single heart to save and love each other or a living thing.

Understand this, that you are part of us and we are part of you no matter what you say or do. We love you all and all we can say is that one day. . . one day. (This is emotional work for us too because of the way *we feel* for you all). Everything will be okay but you must all try to succeed as 'timing' in the sense of the word is so important as we have said in Chapter One.

Earlier we mentioned that so many of you and all living things have wondered that if there is a 'God', why does he not help me/us. Well, if in your heart and what has been read so far in this book has not been quite understood, we ask you to read once again the poem in Chapter Four 'What is Love?'. (This is okay, but because of how you may feel it is important we reiterate it).

One day there is time for you all to cross over to the light, a time mapped out and chosen *before* you were born. You see, life is about learning and about love - two things inseparable and instilled within us by the Creator from when we all first existed.

Imagine for a while (and this will be easier for some because you may have experienced it already), the loss of a loved one, a father, a mother, brother, sister or child. Did they pass over in so much pain? What was the reason for it and why? Why did they experience it and why did *you* experience their pain and hurt and your *loss* or their gain, (or your gain in fact)? (We know some will think that this is nonsense and that you die and when you die - that is it!).

There are two things to perceive with feelings of the Creator when you feel this pain. Many will feel abandoned and confused and others so lost. These are all part of your learning experiences and your search 'within'. We have heard people who say all their lives, "I believe in God, but my newborn son or daughter has been taken away from me and I believe no more. If there was a real 'God' he would have saved him, or her that is for sure. Why did he not help me and my family?"

Look at this from behind the 'scene'. Not easy if the pain and hurt (and which in fact) is (and will) always be with you, because of your love. Why did you lose your child? Why was he/she born and then 'lost'? It was because you were destined to feel this way and the loss, part of your (both of your) experience of 'life'. Your child's life (this time) was brief but never in vain - ever. Would you have loved him (or her) less, or more if he/she had lived a week, a month or a lifetime?

Love is born, everlasting. It is eternal and can never be taken away whether you have experienced if for a second, or a minute, or a day or a lifetime. Please, even if you do not think this is so, just think about this for just a moment today, tomorrow or at some point of your life. One day you will turn and find the strength and love within you of the wonder, the Creator. Then you will *never* look back in your lifetime or with those around you and your family and friends. (PAUSE)

Time is drawing close now David and you have things and work to do. Learn and live and tell. Follow your heart and you will find your true *'work' place.* (Ah ha! - you see, we do *see* - referring to you my son). All will be well in time.

Love to you all. Goodbye with Love, peace, truth from me and us.

ME: Wonderful is an appropriate word for today. Thank you all. Love and light forever! David.

MONDAY 9th OCTOBER 1995 10.25 a.m.

ME: I know that the love and light is within me and around me and I feel the strength, the Creator's strength that carries me forward. Please in love and in light, help those in need. Let this pen flow too so that 'man' can learn and live in truth, love and wisdom always and forever. I feel you so close, I know that the pen will flow. Bless you all, my friends, my guides, teachers and family. . .

COMMUNICATION: Hi David, so good that the pen flows as always. Focusing is so important. To focus on the job in hand, whether it be a person's everyday work or working in love and light. This has always been so as it affects those around you and everything around you too as all are connected as one.

Focus straight and true and those who wish to grow will do so because they will be following their heart in the right way - the only true way. Yes, it can be difficult and circumstances cause or try to derail you. This serves two purposes. One, for you to try to keep on track and two, to also understand the negativity that surrounds you or picks away at the light.

This is why, when you acknowledge your strength and light within you, it is easier to focus and keep on course because the light is and always will be stronger if you know and have acknowledged it in your heart. (PAUSE)

Today 'the wonder' continues, but in a slightly different way. This is the last part before a new chapter begins. The next is of an 'enlightened' experience of many but you will see and write of this next time.

Okay, we have gone through a little of man's perception of wondering of the 'all', the 'Creator' and that of which we are all 'born'. The next part of what we wish to tell you today is about the energy, it's structure, and what sustains the 'Creator'.

We have already stated that we were born of true love - an energy in itself. What is so fascinating for all species is to comprehend what the 'Creator' is. Many have laughed (not at you) in the portrayal of a God in any 'form', e.g., the shape of a man sitting on a throne in his palace, his kingdom. Yet we also have and know that the 'Creator' is everywhere and 'all knowing' and 'all seeing'. This raises so many questions, none less than (or important than) "How can it be so?"

We can only tell you that the 'Creator' is a 'pure' energy of the most beautiful kind. It is a life force in itself yet because of it's fantastic structure and infrastructure it can also be described as just 'is' - is here, is there, is everywhere. This is not a 'pun' or a joke, although some may see it this way. The 'Creator' is Universal and infinite.

We as a 'race' and some others in our progress have experienced things that you could never contemplate but what we are all striving for as even the youngest heart does, is to be in the 'Creator's' hearts 'presence' - it's centre. Even though this is not even possible for us (until we have progressed further) we hope to achieve this and one day it may be possible to do so even though it may be only for the briefest moment. It will be the most satisfying and beautiful moment we hope to experience but we can only wait and see.

What we have said is not to make you feel any less or beneath us. You are not and never have been or will be, *because we are one together*. It is because we wish for you to strive forward and to continue to be the best that you can become.

What we also hope is that we have not confused anyone or anything by what we say. We are striving to become the best we can become too in the love and light and by reaching the 'Creator's' centre for the minute 'time' that we may be allowed (or could possibly expect due to the intensity and energy fields), it does not ever mean that you are no less touched too.

We may sound like a record player stuck in a groove but it is only to prove that the 'Creator' is all and is within all, and also that you can never rest and say "I have ended my search, reached my goal and that's the end". The end of what?

Some people who may say, "I have found my 'God'," do no more but this is where it begins. You may have found light and love within yourself and know and feel the energy and wonder, but if you do no more then it is in vain.

It is by expanding yourself (as we have said before) and giving out light that is the true task of all. The 'Creator', when it gave the millions and millions of strands of itself did not think or feel, 'oh well, now they are born and that is the last bit of control, instruction or direction I will give them all'. The light is forever and forever growing and expanding within and out of everything. (PAUSE)

We spoke earlier of the 'Creator's' structure and infrastructure. It is as small or as large as you would care to perceive so it can be there and here and everywhere all at the same time and this is so. It's energy 'flows' are the most wonderful frequency imaginable and are the highest *beyond anything* that mankind can conceive as vibrations.

We talk of resonance but it all goes far and way beyond that. This is why only when you have reached (or anyone has reached) a certain stage of evolution and progress that you can connect to the 'Creator's' true centre, it's true heart's source.

This is why you will never achieve this on the Earth plane in your present situation or state. Only by raising your whole level of vibration and level of love and light for all the Earth to feel, can you then leave the Earth plane to join the 'cord' of light that is being structured and connected to then ascend to your new home.

It will be there when you are connected with the millions of other species. In this overall love and tremendously sweet, harmonious level of vibration and light you will be able to link and connect with others and then go on to touch and be in the 'Creator's' heart centre. It is truly a most beautiful place and future that awaits those that desire it. We say again, meet the challenges and climb those difficult or easy steps. Open the door and enter your new and true 'pathway' to everlasting peace and love.

'REACH OUT'

Enter - those on the pathway of the truth and love,
Energy - immense, overwhelmingly soft and gentle like a dove.
Light - so bright but not the rays of the sun,
Love - divine, a beauty for each and everyone.

A desire - placed in your heart to open and grow,
A hand - outstretched reaching out now for 'only you know'.
A touch - in peace, truth and sharing harmony,
Help - all around and within your everlasting soul and body.

Growth - an expansion, a search, a one true goal,
Togetherness - a joining of all living things and one bright 'soul'.
A Beauty - it cannot be defined or felt just yet,
The 'Creator' - 'is' always and you will find you've already met.

My son, as you still write more journeys have begun and those that will read this will know that they have or are about to. One day we will describe many things in more detail because we know you have had thoughts in many directions like this. In time my son, in time.

Time today to put the pen down but no need to have sadness or a frown. You all have the strength and your own flow, direction and your destiny you will all know. Be 'still', be safe, all the 'Creator's' children. In love and light and truth always forever. Peace and forever together from us and me. See you soon Davey, hee, hee!

ME: As the last sentence flowed and a tingling sensation overcame me - a normal goodbye? A feeling so weird, 'see you soon *Davey*'. No one has called me that before or have they? Perhaps when I was a child. . . Maybe there is something in store for me, I will trust and wait and see.

Thank you all from my heart and soul to all those around. My love shines for you all and I am here to serve the 'Great Spirit' and those in need.

CHAPTER SEVEN

'AN ENLIGHTENED EXPERIENCE'

WEDNESDAY 11th OCTOBER 1995 11.00 a.m.

ME: I feel/felt you say, "Come and join us. . . " and love and light is all around me and I feel you so close. I am here for you all, forever. Please may we continue. . .

COMMUNICATION: We are here David, connected straight away as always. An opening of a 'channel' direct and through to your heart and of the many who wish to listen and to open up 'within'.

The doorway is always there so it's time to turn the key and push open the door just a fraction or maybe more. Take a look and peep inside to see the light and feel the love, no need now for you to hide. Step forward now and you'll never ever look back for yes, it is your pathway and you are on your own right track. Open minds and hearts are on the right path that you have sought, for you have found the true self and the 'Creator', the love that can't be bought.

Love so beautiful and oh so true for us and for you all. Let us continue and move on today. An 'Enlightened Experience' that we wish to tell, to bring you joy and fill your well. To top it up or fill completely, but you will know whether it is a fact, or just an 'incidentally'.

As the sands of time are blown away and fears and doubts cast aside, many, many civilisations and species of all kinds have learned from within and from their hearts. To move forward and to progress and enter the stage of no more tests and worries and concerns. It is this transition, this change, this alteration that each individual has or must go through. Their 'ENLIGHTENED' experience. We will describe a few to you all, but let us take one thing at a time.

There has been or will be (or currently *is*) a timing for each and all to grow. What is significant is that this moment is also 'timeless' because there is no given or precise time, yet it is there within each of us. A point in each of our lives to open up.

Let us explain this again. Everyone knows inside them (and *has* known) from the beginning of what it is that sustains them and what they really are. This has been this way from the very beginning of Creation, but it is when the individual has acknowledged or accepted this within themselves that their 'enlightened' experience reveals itself to them.

Many people will already have experienced many different things in their lives but there are very few experiences that actually alter them from within. It will be one of beauty of that what has made them gasp in awe at the simplicity of it all.

A touch of a dying friend's hand, a new direction of your love, a new or *true* love on your Earth 'plane', a kiss, your first child or a new beginning. Could it be perhaps, something such as a 'vision' or heavenly light that has touched your heart or mind? The fact that you are all individuals, makes and will make, every new experience different for you all. Not least an 'enlightening' experience which affects and changes your very being and your life. . . (PAUSE)

We would like to describe ours to you. It is many, many hundreds of thousands of your 'Earth years' ago. We have already explained that we have two bodies, one physical and one of light and it is the one of light that awakened us and enlightened us to overall truth and peace and love. We had perceived ourselves only as physical since our beginning/our birth and lived as you do, eating, sleeping and learning, but of course, in very different ways.

There came a time when great conflict and congestion ruled over us and our 'elders' were at such loss. Our evolution span had grown so quickly and where we resided became fraught with problems and it was at this time that things began to happen.

We had our own beliefs and faith that had withstood over such a long time, but these elders knew that there was something else within them and within us all. It was one special elder called 'REMUS' (spell it as it sounds, David) that really led us into the (our) new age. It was he who had his 'enlightened' experience which in effect changed us all and our destiny.

Remus had gone away during a time of deep depression and experienced a visit of 'light'. (This has been passed to us all and was how we grew). What was seen was a presence of a multi-coloured spectrum and feelings that 'radiated' and emanated into Remus' body and soul. The story goes that he at first was so overwhelmed he did not or could not perceive what was going on, in or around him.

Remus stood perfectly still and this tremendous warmth and peace enveloped him and he automatically became part of this energy or force. He could see, but without eyes. He could feel, but without touch. He could speak, but without words and he could 'move' without even a second thought. So the light was and so was he.

Over a period of time, Remus came back and he had experienced things beyond our comprehension. It was and felt magical to us, but of course it was not at all. We were all taught over generations to know that there was a light within us that was part of the 'Creator', our God, your God, everyone's 'God'. It indeed was a tremendous 'gift' because from that point onwards everything changed. This will probably sound like a fairytale to many of you, but it is the truth and from my heart as I tell you this. It is very, very special to us all.

Over the ages, we began to understand this within us and it was from there that our new evolution began. Because we could move at 'will', we could reach the planet nearest to us - our second home (and of course, far beyond) and this is how we became known as the TWO 'SISTERS' STAR GROUP. It was like we had this second home - a *twin*. The planet was perfect. It could sustain us and our future growth, no overcrowding or conflict.

The 'light' brought peace and love to us all and enabled us to expand in knowledge and wisdom and love beyond comprehension. We can go anywhere but will always regard where we are as our home until the day when we can remain in the Creator's presence of beauty and love forever.

David, with this new gift came so much love that when we were able to use and share it, it was the most amazing feeling ever. I could be standing somewhere and become light - pure light - pure consciousness in an instant because we are in tune with what is the Creator and what is everything. It is truly wonderful.

Also, in the light and this love came our new responsibility and our new 'goal' for completion as our destiny had altered and changed. It is like (as we have said before), that destiny can only be altered in one way, that is in love, the light and the energy. True love.

We knew from Remus and his awakening (and from then on within us all), that we had to change to succeed. However the work is never or cannot be complete without every connection rejoining together. Yours, mankind's and those in every galaxy of existence.

We are fortunate that others have also been able to help along the way, each with their own individual 'gifts' of love and wisdom to share on every world or home.

It is time to all be enlightened and to experience your awakening. Both global and personal for everyone to join together. Much work, so much work to be done but like us, you can and you will succeed. (For those that wish to.)

As you each go about your everyday lives, please listen, feel and think about those around you and of everything living. The 'time' is within you all and each will be triggered by something different as said before. A voice, a song, a film, a book, a picture or perhaps a touch of a hand.

Only you will know and only you can grow in your way that you will know is right for you. You are all unique (never forget that) in character, shape and size, but inside you are 'one' and are all the same.

We are glad David, to share in a piece of our history although very short and brief. Time for you to go, 'your work' to do and the experience to continue when the pen flows again. Love and truth and peace, from me and us to you all. Goodbye for now.

ME: Thank you from my heart. Goodbye, too.

FRIDAY 13th OCTOBER 1995 10.30 a.m.

ME: My love must be forever strong, taking me, carrying me and sustaining me through life's ups and downs. Sometimes when I am weak and let darkness in. It is difficult to overcome, but I know that I *will* win, by always turning within. . .

COMMUNICATION: Come to the light, knock on the door and push it open as we have said before. It is always there, waiting for you and all those who wish it. Acknowledge the light and share in your new experience that may change your life - for a day, or forever, only you will know.

Yes, 'experiences' to continue today because within them lies a pathway in itself. Everything is an experience for you, from when you are reborn on to the Earth 'plane' until it is time for you to return. When you think about it, you do learn so much don't you, but some things of course are more important than others.

You may look back to childhood. Your first step (or crawl), the first word (or noise) spoken, "Mummy or Daddy" and your first ride on a bicycle or trip to a fairground. Know that your first year's of growth, being nurtured (or sometimes neglected) by your parents and family are so very important.

As you get older you seek to stretch out your hand for understanding and knowledge with good or bad results, but it does not matter as long as you have been true to yourself and those around you who love and care for you. Life is for learning and living, but remember to live in the right way always.

Things are always natural and not forced. They have always been this way and always shall and so is the learning process. When you seek to strive forward and try to push too hard and too fast, be patient, because what you are really learning or experiencing may not ever be rushed. Everything as it should be and always 'cause and effect' - that effect follows the cause.

When the child puts it's hand into the flame, it burns and hurts. It rushed to seek and find out for itself - curiosity. The flame was fire and it knew no different and it could not think, "Oh this is a child so I will not burn it!" Fire is fire, obviously. But simplicity is the message and of course within yourself you know the answers to *all* your questions.

However, whether it is a helping hand from someone who has gained information through their own experiences and passed those on to you, or if you have taught or understood yourself, it does not matter. There is no quick or right way but only the truth in all that you seek and all that you do and learn.

How many times have you desired the short cut, the quick route and it has backfired on you? As we have said before, look deeper and see the cause of 'why' it had happened to you. Do not say, "Why not him or her?" (Hard to do this we know sometimes).

We are not saying things such as you should be trodden on or pushed aside and just accept it, but to look beyond the 'event' and the circumstances and your situation. In every loss there is a potential gain. A learning or 'enlightened' experience and not in just a materialistic sense. Feel it, live it and LEARN from it.

When you fail the test, or do not get the job you so hoped and desired for or missed out on a golden opportunity, try thinking of something different instead of the 'why not!' Think from within and think 'why' or 'because'. . .

Everything you achieve or do not achieve or experience would have and will have an effect on you and all around you. So as this is so maybe it is because you need to learn more or understand the lesson before passing the test. No short cuts but hard work.

Would that job have had other effects? Was it for you, or for others that you wanted the job? Maybe you did not need the promotion. Maybe you did not need the money or maybe you did not need the stress for you or for the family around you. Perhaps it was saying that you should be content? We would never say that you should not strive to be the best that you can or could become, but it is the experience of 'this' what we wish to explain to you.

Perhaps the golden opportunity was a rich reward or a change to go and travel. "It was mine! My chance, my one chance to escape from myself and all that I know that is my situation or difficulties at this point of my life". Have these things ever happened to you?

Search inside yourself and your past and link something to that negative situation, (or *you* may think it was negative at the time). What did you learn from it, experience from it? Pleasure or pain - a gain?

You can never cheat or lie to yourself. Oh you may try but although you may succeed outwardly, inside you can never hide from your true 'self', your higher self, your consciousness, your Soul, your Spirit. It is you and all that sustains you.

In time you have to face all what you need to learn. So if you move and 'escape' from your problem, who is there to say that you will not have to face it again later and it may be stronger - deeper rooted next time. . . Face up always to the experience. Live it, breathe it and try to understand it for it is yours and your experience alone. (Never forget that you can overcome *everything* with love. The love that is within yourself and from others - it is there always).

So you see, what we have said today is of 'experiences'. Some would say, "Yes, but these are not enlightened experiences. They are not of life changing beliefs or visions of religion(s)". We never said they were. Who says that an experience, an 'enlightened' experience is one or the other. You are all different and as this is so, what one person sees, hears, feels, touches, tastes, or instinctively goes through, will/may be different, (but not always so). It is in the person's mind that they put definitions or boundaries on these things, not us. What could be an 'enlightened' experience to someone could mean nothing to another and vice versa.

Maybe one day a crossroads in a person's life is met and straight over, he/she goes, onwards forwards and tirelessly striving towards their 'goal'. Does he/she get there any quicker? What would have happened if they had gone left or right, could this have led them there to it even faster? Or had they been moving so quick that their goal and their desire was already there, but they had passed it by in their rush.

Perhaps you sometimes need to take a backwards step to find what you are looking for, or a backwards step to move forward! What would have been there on the left turn or the right, more information, more direction? Only *you* can ever know whilst you are there to learn. If you take the wrong turning, perhaps you needed to experience the change of direction or the 'side' event.

No matter though, because eventually you will all get to where you need to be. Enjoy your life and it's experiences and those feelings and senses you have from them for they will carry you forward either sooner or later, depending on whether you can understand them. Listen to the effect in your heart. It is through this that 'all' will progress to the overall 'enlightened' experience that awaits mankind and to those of truth and love and peace. (PAUSE)

Time is drawing close again David and we have to prepare for something else and for others in a new direction. We will explain one day of this. Till the pen flows again my son and continuation begins again. (No not a new chapter, just an expression.) A little more of experiences to follow.

Love to you all in peace, truth, love and harmony. From us all and me, goodbye.

ME: Goodbye from me too. (N.B: It is amazing that when I re-read what has come through today, it relates to so many of the things that I have (and friends and family have) gone/or are going through. I hope this love and wisdom gives you strength when you face difficult times that you may be going through, either now or in the future.) Thank you.

SUNDAY NIGHT 15th OCTOBER 1995

ME: Before you read *Monday's* communication I need to share an 'experience' from last night, which occurred before I went to bed. Here are some brief notes.

It was 10.30 p.m. and I said a prayer whilst on the landing looking out of the window at the stars. Such a clear night and the constellation of the Plough (the Great Bear, the Big Dipper) was just to the right, over the chimney breast on the extension of the house.

I asked, "Would it be too much to ask to see something, a comet or a shooting star, perhaps?" (I had recently on three occasions been fortunate to be in the right place at the right time to see two shooting stars and a comet.

Beautiful sights indeed).

I waited for about half a minute and I thought 'never mind, not to worry' and as I then began to turn away. . . Far in the distance was a brilliant white light, slightly coloured (blurred) and dull underneath. My recognition of it lasted about a second, then it shot from right to left and downwards at a slight angle for about another second or so and then it just disappeared! Not a comet, not a shooting star, but. . . ?

I got into bed and thought about what I had seen and as I lay there, asked in my mind 'was it either of those things?'. Nothing replied, then I received a very strong 'vibration' of 'yes' when I asked, "Was it a UFO?" I felt at the time (and of course, this was before I received the communication the next morning), that my friends were just saying "Hi!". . .

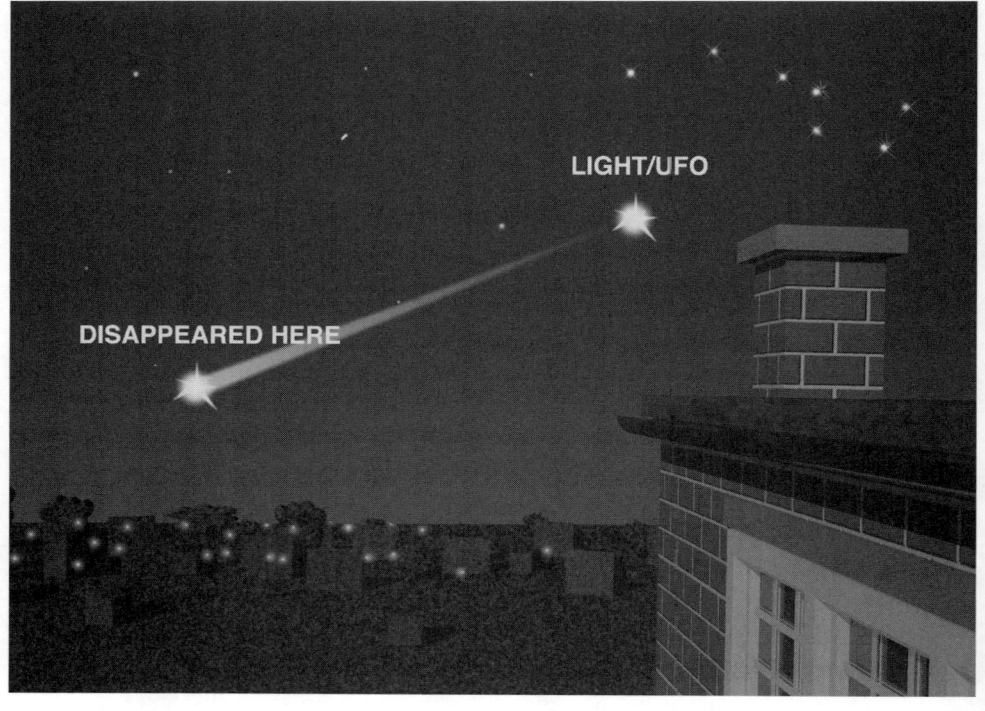

PICTURE FIFTEEN: 'HELLO!.... UFO'

View from 'Landing' Window

Obviously this is difficult to portray to anyone, because people may say "Okay, how big? What colour? What shape?" It was just so fast, there wasn't any time. . . but it *did* happen. There is nothing on this earth that could be so 'static' in the night sky like that and then move across the distance as it did and with such speed that this 'object' had and just disappear.

I have just thought as I write, that maybe someone, somewhere also saw 'something' that night or wether it was even picked up on radar. (Military or commercial). Who knows, maybe someone could let me know as it would be extra proof, not that I need it. Incredible.

P.S. Maybe this experience was 'that' which was meant by "See you soon, Davey." (On Oct 6th 1995), or could it be another experience to follow?

MONDAY 16th OCTOBER 1995 10.40 a.m.

ME: Heavenly Father, the Great Spirit, our 'Creator', all of my friends and family, teachers and guides, I feel so much better since the weekend. I feel closer, if that is even possible and I feel stronger in my heart. Thank you for the messages over the last few days and the 'experience' last night. They were all lovely.

Please let us continue this last part (?) of Chapter Seven, an 'enlightened experience'. I hope the pen flows and the 'light' put on to paper for all to see and read. Bless you from my heart. . .

COMMUNICATION: Hi David! You saw a glimpse of 'something'* last night and we could see you as you gazed in delight. So fast, so silent, do you not agree, to get to one world from another, to 'see'. (NB: One of various 'physical' method's)

So you asked and so you saw and we listen to your heart for always, not only just the once more. 'Believe' and you will know in time of what there is to 'grow'. Patient and patience are two traits, but one of the same - nothing too long to wait in vain. Be still, be still and grow as one for you will as many, shall become.

Well, let us conclude Chapter Seven as you have rightly said and the 'enlightened experience'.

Has it been taught, or said, or been inbred? An individual will only know which by what is inside of them and when it clicks into place. This is personal

*The Light/UFO

growth and understanding for development on their pathway to the permanent love and permanent light.

Today, we ask a question directed at 'you' who reads this. Will you seek to find and learn? Or will you listen to the question, then cast it aside not to know? A choice, a personal one, a very private one between your heart, your life and your higher self and your soul. . . where the answer lies, within.

Some may feel that their experience is never to be known or hidden (and this can be true) but if you never seek how can you possibly find out so that you may grow. Look for a teacher (yourself 'within' of course) or maybe someone you find that thinks the same. Possibly someone who can listen to your heart and help your true self and not for a material gain. . . (PAUSE)

We seem to see that in each of you there is a different goal. Some follow that to the end with such fervour and so painstakingly and methodically until the realisation or achievement. A doctorate or perhaps even a travel plan to climb the highest mountain or to walk the length and breadth of a country. All these are important to the individual of course and part of their life and experiences. They may then feel elated beyond belief, "I have achieved something that no other has done and that makes me special!"

Yes indeed, a great personal achievement perhaps has been achieved and nothing can take that away from you, ever. But realise as we have said, you are all special and you each can achieve what is in your heart if it is strong enough. For example.

1. If everyone took up the same challenge of peace and love with their 'desire' as strong as their goals then wouldn't you all have achieved something that could never be surpassed?

2. The desire needs to be as strong as a single individual's, to create the 'overall' experience.

Imagine the person who sets out to pass their one desire and there are many, many, many 'famous' people who have done this on your 'Earth plane'. You can look back into history, (we do not need to recite them to you), when the task seemed too great and they were on their own - (in a physical sense) - did they give up? When they looked out over the horizon and were lost, did they crawl into a ball and think, 'I can't go on'?

Let us tell you *many* have thought these things, but when they have got to the time of judgement of character, a belief of sheer determination and courage, they turned 'within' themselves. A power, an experience so strong, so beautiful, that most could not describe. This carried them, this directed them, this sustained them so that they become what they 'became'.

Every single one of you has 'it' within you. A light so bright and it is only when you wish to discover it and experience it that it will flourish. When you know this and understand it, all the things achieved by mankind and the individual, pale into comparison. (BUT IN NO WAY BELITTLING THOSE WHO HAVE ACHIEVED THAT BY SHEER GUTS AND TALENT AND FROM WITHIN THEMSELVES).

The experience is there and you will feel 'enlightened' but always when it is true. No false pretences or half gestures as these will not see you through or help others. If those 'famous' people had only been half-hearted then do you think that they would have surpassed and achieved their desires or goals or even in some cases, survived? Love and light will show you the way always, for tomorrow, the future and today. Seek it, share it, believe in it and you *will* know what we have described both forever in your heart and in helping all and mankind.

Let us make it clear that we have never said 'must' and 'or else'. It is down to you and you the individual alone. We do not ask for you to give all your money away or to go on the street in rag clothes, (that would be up to you) but to do what is right in your heart and to help each other in small ways. A helping hand to lift someone from the ground in love and peace says so much.

You do not have to run or shout or preach night and day to give someone love or to light up their day. Everything in all of your hearts is connected in love and energy forever. Reach, just reach and touch it and you will never look back. (PAUSE)

Well it is up to each of you to ask the question or moreover to find your answer thats yours alone. Discuss in friendship with your 'neighbour' or your 'brother' and gain in wisdom and knowledge where you can but always the truth is inside and can be given out with your heart's open hand.

Experience is life and life is experience. Experience can be plain or an 'enlightened' one. Which will yours be? Will it be good and so much fun, or just part of 'living' and in darkness? Maybe with hate or shame, to fight or use a gun. . . taking aim?

Go where you will and do what you feel. Follow the truth and you will not go far wrong. It could be a new start, a new beginning or it may have already begun. You know it is within you and is your choice,. You can live in peace and harmony and you will become. . . Please live and trust and everything will flow in due course. Whether it is fast or slow, you can and will succeed if you open up to YOUR EXPERIENCE. You will *know* it and you will *feel* it.

Well David, yes it is time to move on. Two thirds of the way there, in this the first one? Much work to do and you will see there's much to collate and piece together and you will do this well. Okay! Chapter Eight next time the pen flows and it is called 'DEBATE'.

You 'think' along the right lines. A 'for and against' or points of view, an argument or just plain news? You will see and understand. Debate in time and to lend a hand. Goodbye in truth, peace and love from me and us. . .

David, as always in your heart do trust. Things are on course, it is okay. Completion date, no need to worry as this will be reached in 'time and finance' as has been said before. Love, till next time and as always, take care. Goodbye.

ME: Phew!. . . it's funny sometimes, I'm not sure what to say. . . love and light to you too, this day.

CHAPTER EIGHT

'DEBATE'

FRIDAY 20th OCTOBER 1995 10.40 a.m.

ME: I look forward to this, 'our' time, when the pen 'flows' so much. I feel you near and open my heart to hear and feel your love in every direction for each and every nation. Praise be to the Great Spirit, our 'Creator'. Welcome to my friends and family once more.

COMMUNICATION: We are here my son. We know what you have gone through over the last few days and of your feelings and thoughts. Some difficult times, but you will pull through as you have the trust from 'within'. You will see and you will win just as we have said to you before.

Chapter Eight . . . 'DEBATE'. Could it all be something to listen to then heed or acknowledge or instead be cast out and aside, wanting hate and greed?

There are many viewpoints one could take to begin with this and also many 'time frames' of your history and of other civilisations too. One thing at a time though.

We thought of the beginning and decided to incorporate some of these viewpoints to start it with. Is this not a debate in itself you may ask. Just as there are two sides to a coin and two sides to every story or agreement and moreover a disagreement, then this is where we will try to explain our feelings and information first.

Okay, what we have discussed and explained to you from page one of this book concerns you all, but some will say, "does it?" Likewise, to those that open to all we have said there will also be those that will throw the book onto the fire and discount us as 'incorrect, misguiding' or even the 'darkness'. We cannot see why.

We have always found this on our pathway and destiny in helping others to reach their own 'ascension' level - that of this 'internal' and 'external' debate. What we mean by this is that there will also be two sides, not just around you and everyday life, but also within yourself as you try to turn 'within' to your *'true self'*.

Self doubt? Uncertainty? Confusion in the change of belief or feelings that will envelope you and guide you in new directions? So you see, there is so much more to a straightforward 'Debate'. Is it two sides or more?

Is it two sets of feelings or two people or two families, two towns, two nations, heading to friction or decay, or could it light the way?

Yes, it indeed throws many interesting aspects to the fore does it not and can get one thinking in all sorts of directions. Let us return to the 'two sides'. In time there will be debates, possibly about this book and others like it and you may have closed minds in one corner and 'open' in the other. This is sad but often inevitable in a search for truth or believability in being 'whole' or in following a faith.

We expect this. A comparison if you like between religions and of what we say, because it is natural and we have seen it many times and in many ways on many planets. Sometimes it is in larger, much larger scales of bureaucracy or in governing bodies, but sometimes too, it is so small in conflict that it is over almost as it has begun. (Those are wonderful to see - a realisation born and understood very quickly). Only time, your time will reveal your outcome to all.

We can picture this now, a stage, a television documentary or chat show where 'debate' is thorough and very to the point. But, no matter what is ever discussed or argued at the finger point, those that see, listen and hear the two sides will learn something new and it will pose a question even in the staunchest mind of a closed individual. (By the way, we do not say or mean that it is condemning someone who is closed but reiterate that by experiencing or following new lines of thought, they perhaps could or would open up to so much more. Maybe they can, or you will.)

Always in your lives we see this 'head to head' when conflict of opinions strikes and it may seem like it is inevitable or necessary but it isn't. Whether it be in a family or neighbourly dispute or even worldwide, everything, every single problem can be worked out if there is the give, not 'take' and the sharing.

So the parties, the two people or the two countries, (sometimes more we know), who have much diverse and hated opinions of each other need to relax their anger and do more than debate. (PAUSE)

Debate is a small word really but can be a million miles apart in thinking of these different feelings and viewpoints. There has to be an understanding and a connection between the two sides involved and by opening up, this can be achieved. (Such a simple statement, but so hard to follow in times of conflict).

We hope, we guarantee in fact, that there will be at least one connection to every single individual who reads this book. It may be a single word (as we have said before) or a picture, a poem, a chapter or even the front cover. It is this one connection that can lead to the understanding and the opening up of even closed or negative viewpoints or disbelief deep down inside an individual.

In every word spoken by another there is a truth. Even minute details that many cannot see or understand. The debate can lead to saying 'okay this is new, this is different or this is just so false', but no matter what first thoughts or arguments are put across in maybe discounting it, or casting it aside, it will have touched an inner part of you.

This may be forgotten on the outside, but inside, etched in the memory forever. So. . . by reading it, digesting it, and more so by being so close to the debate or discussion, you have subconsciously involved yourself, your mind, your very being, to comprehend now or at some later stage in your life. Utter rubbish? We will, and you will see.

What will be interesting is 'man's' thirst for the discussion and the debate to continue and where it will lead. Yes the understanding, but there is no ending, there isn't one.

On the Earth plane, even when decisions have been made and conflicts and debates settled, there is very often underlying currents of confusion. Perhaps bitterness or division between the ranks of the common people. This is because in the hearts of those that the debates concern, all is not concluded. This is so very much the core of many problems, these hidden feelings and their emotions.

Some people may say they are happy to keep the status quo, but are boiling angry underneath. This is why centuries old wars or conflicts re-emerge into bitter feuds and battles once more - because their debate returns to *hate*. (PAUSE)

There is a progression we see and the 'light' expanding that if sufficient, will change all this to succeed in 'ascension'. We are sure that as many more people turn 'within' from the outer wrongs and rights and the confusion and the debates to concentrate on themselves when the difficult problems and arguments arise, then perhaps a peaceful solution, a permanent one will be found. The two 'sides' again being in harmony and in conjunction with the same desires and everlasting goal.

As your time passes we will watch the many doors open to those that wish to enter. The Great Spirit, our 'Creator' does not ever shut the door in the face of truth, of love and of peace. Over your many centuries, (this time around) much power on one side has shut the door to those in need - those in hunger and of those who are suffering.

It is now that the common people of all nations need to unite and show their hand and tell their side of the story. To share their grief at the hardship and pain that they go through is not fair. It is time for those in 'control' to listen to them or they will fall in their own demise, their own 'gain' and their own misused power.

There will always be those who are poor and rich and each have their own views and struggles, but now is the dawning of new thinking. It is for each and every single one of you to search and question your own motives of life and of living. It is now time that the world (the whole world) needs to debate on the truth and the love for humanity and every living being, be it man, woman, child, animal, insect, plant or the elements. (Life forces in themselves).

We shall see what all have to say. To listen and embark in the correct way, the correct journey or to hold on to indifference and to fight and permanently stay. We have seen this before and we know that LOVE will prevail, but the burning question is when?. . . (PAUSE).

Well David, today is due to close till next time. We know that we have come across quite strongly but perhaps those that read this will relate to us this way. Aren't 99% of your earthly debates like this? Turn on practically every television station across your globe, open every newspaper and you can find it this way. This is why we knew that this first part had to be of such an attitude, because most will realise this and in their hearts too.

Okay, it is time to go and we hope you have grown just a little bit more. Never forget we care about you all and you are always in our hearts, whether we are near or afar. Take care and do and be the best you can be today and always. Goodbye, love and truth in peace from me and us. . .

ME: Thank you all for being within and surrounding me. You are always part of the love that is around me with such love and peace I cannot describe. You will always be part of the light in my life. Goodbye to you all.

MONDAY 23rd OCTOBER 1995 6.40 p.m.

ME: Even though I am unwell, I know that you are within and around me. Praise be to the 'Great Spirit'. Please let this pen flow as my heart flows forever in your love and light. N.B: (As I started to write it was like the candle has somehow given out *twice* as much light! It is so bright, thankyou.)

COMMUNICATION: We are here my son and we know that sometimes all your hearts weigh with the trouble and strife and ills of the Earth plane and those stresses of your everyday existences.

All ills usually start from within and friends have said to you in the past, they (the illnesses) can be a cleansing out process. A cleansing of the heart and mind and soul which is often a personal goal in itself.

Maybe one day, all will realise that when the time is right, there will be no illness and pain. No hunger, no stress and no animosity or hate towards anything. This will *'become'* - make no mistake of that! It is just. . . what ills or pain does or will each of you go through to strive forward in your heart or mind to achieve it? (It is a personal choice and outcome that one).

Okay, well let us continue the 'Debate' and proceed to move on from where we last left off. We hope you'll find this part intriguing David, and of course all those too who will read and possibly feel inside themselves what we are trying to put across to you.

There was a time in our history when we were faced with a massive choice or debate. It does not matter what you call it, either word will do, because in our case it was one of the same. Yes indeed, we had to come to a decision that meant either a forwards or backwards step in our progress and evolution. I know that we have recently said that eventually, if you took an incorrect pathway or road you would still end up where you wanted to be - and possibly wiser - but with us this was different.

This choice and debate was imperative to us because it affected, or more significantly would affect, so much more than ourselves as well as those 'beings', those creatures on many planets and civilisations that followed and would follow our example and outcome. In a way it was an 'acceptance' and although this word is very straightforward and would seem simple to comprehend, it went way, way beyond this.

To describe it is quite difficult, because to portray to you all the feeling of anticipation and what would be the 'knock on' effect was immense to say the least. We were at a point of our evolution where certain leaders and principals of 'government' were very fixed in how things were done and run. This included the way we lived, travelled and underwent new learning and procedures of understanding together with the consequences it had on each and every individual and as a 'collective'.

When we inherited new dimensions of light and knowledge (and subsequent wisdom that came with it) from the teachings of Remus that were handed down from generation to generation, there came a point where some felt beyond or more capable, or in a sense more independent than they actually were. We knew that each individual had the right to their opinions and expressions (as you all do on Earth) but this went too far.

Part of our civilisation (and we reiterate that this was a very, very long time ago) in effect broke away from, or side tracked its inner wealth of togetherness and 'oneness' thinking that they had it all! As if they 'knew this and knew that' of the new information to control beyond what was known as the 'tier of light infrastructure' which the 'Creator' had given us to follow. In a sense it was a little bit similar (the nearest thing we would guess) to certain requests, not rules or commandments but a sort of code of conduct in a way.

This at first caused a fraction - two sides, two viewpoints, two choices for our people and hence the 'debate' began. Most people who read this may now think "Ah, there must have been a war which followed", but this was not the case. Because of such diversity, those that wanted too went to our second planet to live with their differences to find their own success or failure and growth.

It was so sad as we did not interact as a species for many millennium even though we were so close (in distance). Even *we* could diverse and have a 'split'. So much heartache, pain and confusion, but hope and prayer was evident for a long time to rectify this.

We know that this may sound like so much conjecture, but how can we elaborate on this at this stage when *we* cannot be sure you will be able to follow or understand it. One day though perhaps soon.

We said earlier that so much depended on us. We were like a testing ground - not a 'guinea pig' - but a huge emphasis on unity or togetherness and it was placed upon us to see if our light can/could become 'one' again after a long period of 'fractioning'.

After this period came the 'breakaways' return caused by its own inner self experiencing a higher light - a signal by the 'Creator' itself to the hierarchy there. They expanded and they accepted what was there all the time (but could not see it) a frequency of such beauty and magnitude, the immense wonder of such peace.

The debate was over and of course we had open arms for our own 'family', our own sisters, brothers and children. What occurred next was of unbelievable proportions to what any of us had ever experienced. Due to the coming together of two planet's frequencies, a channel of vibrant power, a flux and a burst of light was given out between the two. Both planets were encompassed in a brilliant white, yellow and gold aura that was never piercing but it was like being bathed in the sweetest, softest, elegant glow. It was so beautiful.

It was like being touched by so much love (*and POWER*), we all (and every living thing) opened our hearts. It was at this point, this one point in our entire history and evolution that *finally* convinced us all. Everyone and everything.

When you can touch, smell, taste, hear, see and be in a love like that, it was as if you did not exist but you did, such a marvellous (and wonderful) thing.

Picture this if you can. Inside this energy, this love, we had no cares, no despair, no hate, no conflict, no *debates*. We were together, infused as one family. NO differences, just. . . love and appreciation that is so hard to even think of or compare with anything else really. It is this that is our goal. Our destiny to be in the 'Creator's' heart's centre once again at a higher level. We can only achieve this if we fulfill our task and our destiny to help you, mankind and the millions of others too. You are just one of many but are unique and precious too and we will do our best, but we pose a question, a choice - a debate. Will YOU?

After our experience and the aura faded, it was like there were invisible lines of connection to our other planet - our sister planet. Each our second homes now to live and share and always be as one.

Once this happened, many other civilisations came to see what had been and was taking place. Their own experiences followed and so the journey began for others. A 'knock on' effect from galaxy to galaxy, from star to star, home to home, love uniting not diversing. (PAUSE)

It is when you have all achieved and passed your debate and your choices to 'ascend' on the precious cord of light being formed as we communicate, (although a small fragment of course at this stage), that you will be in the correct place for everlasting truth and peace.

Please do not misunderstand what we say here. You know as many do, that the planes of existence are infinite - too numerous to count - but where it is that mankind will truly call home is the 'plane' of *COMMUNITY*.

Why have we been so direct and so explicit? It is because of your growth. Over your millennium you have and will have (when you 'ascend'), become specific in a certain 'area' of harmonisation. In a way and in a sense 'special' (although you already are) to others, for the way your love will radiate from you. All other species will, for two reasons be able to relate and COMMUNICATE to you and through you;

1) Because you will all be in the 'Creator's' peace and harmony of the truth.
2) Because of the *love* that you are, or rather <u>will</u> become.

There is such a complexity to all of this information and sheer expansion of it, that any more at this time would not be fair to you. As the light grows all around and within you so much more will be understood by many and when the moments in your new history are designated, you will be ready for them and you will *know*. (PAUSE)

Remember when you were a child with a complex sum you may have had to do, but your brain could not take it in. Now you are older and wiser, if you had the same sum now, it would be. . . 'child's play'. *Therefore* everything in it's time. Remember too, a friend of yours once said "YOU CANNOT LEARN ANY MORE THAN THE LEVEL YOU HAVE REACHED!" (We thought that would make you laugh).

Well David, time for you to go as the last part of 'debate' is for when the pen is ready to flow again. Remember the individual has a choice and personal feelings. Only the individual can 'become' and go one way or the other, or just sit on the fence too.

Love to you all, always. The 'Creator' is in us and you and in all things. Seek the truth and the light and your love will give and be in your life. Goodbye, truth, peace and us. Please. . . in yourself do trust.

ME: I could feel my body tingle all over with energy. Wonderful. Thank you all from my heart.

THURSDAY 26th OCTOBER 1995 9.45 a.m.

ME: Dear Father, my family, friends, teachers and guides within and around me. Protect me, (as always), guide me and teach me so that I may help others. Always in life, in light, in love and peace and harmony, let this communication flow so that we may all grow.

My hope and my trust is with you all, always. I feel so alone sometimes yet am never alone because you are here and around us, never to part.

We are 'one' forever and until we raise our frequencies know that we will not reach our true home. Bless you all. Your son and learning child - David.

COMMUNICATION: The light is around you my son and you all. We will always reiterate this until you all understand in your hearts and souls and minds.

We know that as your time goes by, you face your challenges and growth with different attitudes and attributes that are within you. Some are overcome easily and some quite painfully but keep going in the right direction that your hearts take you, for it is the will, it is the way - your destinies.

Keep trusting and your heart's love and light will carry you over the obstacles that crop up in each of your daily lives. Wherever you go, whoever you are, there is someone who can help you and guide you and direct you both on your Earth plane and other planes too. You may feel alone, but we can assure you, oh, please be well assured. . . you are never, ever, ever alone.

Love is infinite as we have said. It holds no boundaries. So even in your darkest hour there is love and light to be seen, to be felt and to be touched. Open always to this truth and this will be found and then you can succeed in your goals, your desires, your hopes for mankind and the animal kingdom and for every living thing. Nothing too great if unity is there and you have all shared. (PAUSE) (Bless you too, my son.)

Well, let us move on and complete this Chapter Eight - Debate. Imagine for a moment a huge and deep 'well'. At first, two things could come to mind; perhaps a well of water or a well of oil? Now suppose something else instead. Imagine in your mind the leader of every nation; of each and every race of mankind, from East, West, North and South, standing beside the well like an open mouth.

Once upon a time, people threw a coin into a well and made a wish or held a hand or gave someone a kiss. What do you think would happen if every leader stood by a well at this very second in time? Could they, or would they link arms or could they even turn their backs on one another?

There is we see, a summit going on - your 'UNITED NATIONS' - some of your leaders make a mockery of this word and they may laugh and joke, but should take it far more seriously. Not just for themselves, but for those that are not even present.

'United' or divided? Maybe *they* should all consider their choice, their debate, in more detail below their 'agenda' and stop scratching the surface and listen. To open their ears and eyes and look at the effect their decisions have on all things and not their individual requirements or necessities or gains.

Perhaps one day all leaders will really be at the well. A well of hope and kindness and inside it crystal clear water . . . , but not water. Perhaps it will be filled with tears of joy and emotions, or maybe it will be full of darkness and hate and they can then preside over what calamity they have inflicted on you all. (This of course, we sincerely hope does not happen, and if you all live in the way of truth and love, it will not).

We know that if they all come together in peace, it will not be a single coin falling into the well. If the correct choices are made and the debates of you all are concluded from the heart, what you will see, and more importantly 'feel', is a heavenly star falling from afar. A beautiful golden light, lighting up the night. It will fall into the well of your souls, the well of your emotions and tears, but it will never be extinguished or covered over. It will shine eternally.

What we are asking and requesting, is that you all come to the well of love, hope, truth and the light and to make your choice to live not fight. You may be no leader of a country or nation, but can do more for life, your life, other's lives than you ever imagined.

ME: There was a pause in the communication right here. Then such stillness, peace and tranquility overcame me. After a while (how long I do not know), I could sense energy rushing through me as the connection of love came through my mind.

Somehow I knew that a poem was to be written down. . . to guide us all.

'THE WELL'

Deep within you, is the flame that holds no blame,
a light so so beautiful, inside it has no pain.
And there is a well, around this in your heart,
it has many layers too, but not made of fragile parts.

It holds you where you are so you can grow and learn,
until the special day, when on your way back home.
Do not look internally, to the black or darkness of the oil,
just look around instead and feel life's glowing, radiating coil.

Cast a coin out wide, to make your wish for all mankind,
make it true and not in value, of the penny or the dime.
In each and every crystal and every source of light,
is the energy to sustain and make things true and right.

So be you and be true, to the living things of this world,
or will the feelings so deep remain, and the story stay untold.
So give way to whatever, is holding you all back,
dive deep into your well and never, ever look back.

Love is there forever, for each of you and all,
no matter what shape or size or whether you're tall or small.
And whether you can't talk or whether you can't see,
you are always surrounded by, the love and truth and beauty.

Now go and link your hands, of a clear and true friendship,
more action and less talk to end all pain and hardship.
Uncover now the well, of your precious heart,
then you will understand. . . that we never, ever part.

My son, your love is strong and we see this so much. Regain your *bodily* strength for there is much to do. You have it within you so your search for good and helping others will continue as your light shines bright and oh, so true. Find others in the light and join together and the stronger you will all become. Then shed the light far and wide and push this darkness and the grey aside to seek the love that is you and you all, as we keep saying.

David, your 'peace' is drawing near and you will be able to do so much more of that what you wish to do and serve. Patience and patients are very similar words, as we have recently said to you.

Time to go now and the next chapter is nine. Is it yours, ours, mine or mankind's? Chapter Nine is about the wait and the frustration, and this is why we have called it 'DELIBERATION'.

Goodbye my son, from me and us. Love to you all, in truth, peace and in light do trust.

ME: Thank you to *all* my friends and my family. My love is for you always.

CHAPTER NINE

'DELIBERATION'

MONDAY 30th OCTOBER 1995 10.45 a.m.

ME: Dear Father, help me to put my differences aside. Help me to help myself as I must, as all comes from 'within' oneself to achieve and not to deceive. The illness and darkness must go so that my light may shine for others to see and show your love, light and beauty that is within everything.

Please guides, teachers and friends of every single 'plane' of existence, watch over me. I pray, please help me get through these days. My heart and yours are always one together - praise the 'Great Spirit' our 'Creator'. . .

Please may I have one more small clue?* Am I lazy in asking for this? Maybe it will be revealed in my mind as I work through this new information. . . 'DELIBERATION'.

COMMUNICATION: Well my son, as the flame draws higher as our frequencies meet, we see you awake and when you are asleep. As the light shines through each and every 'plane', yes, we do wish you to know our name. Although you have tried to solve our game, in scratching the surface you've come close but not in vain.

Many things and answers are wanted by many of you and who is to say that what is important to one person, is to another. An answer to a simple question is all that an individual may need to change their life.

Others may require pages and pages to convince or quench their mind's 'thirst' for proof or for completing their objective thoughts to one of single mindedness.

Before we begin DELIBERATION David, we have decided amongst us to let you *see* another clue in your mind. Your thoughts at this very second are not too far behind so we think that in your heart you already know our name

---

*For 'Their' Name

anyway . . . As you have always, all along! Close your eyes for a moment and be still. We will want you do draw a picture(s) of what you see and experience, and then it 'described' for others. . .

ME: How long this lasted I do not really know, but this was unbelievable - such peace and love - immense. . .

A 'ball' of light like a glowing 'sun'. Brilliant yellow and gold rays, piercing, but I could 'see'.

My mind became a part of this light (as if in the light) at such speed and movement across an ocean. Then I stopped.

Such peace and silence over the sea. Two dolphins came from the surface and leapt high with such beauty and elegance, as if 'free'. The 'light' seemed to pass through them, higher and higher until it was in 'Space'. It then looked down upon the Earth and lines of brilliant light started spiralling, radiating outwards in different directions, as if they were lines of travel, movement and communication.

Suddenly it was as if I, my mind in the light, was on a craft, a ship. I could sense and see such clear images. First a feeling that to the left was part of the 'drive' system including pipes, components of the 'propulsion'. (Some sort of a room.) I could see a 'figure' moving away from this but not walking, as if half light, half physical.

Then, in another area a 'misty' image of a figure at some sort of control panel, half lying down, then proceeded forward in movement. (Picture Sixteen: 'A JOURNEY' page 123)

A pause, very brief, followed. Suddenly I saw a 'bee' sitting on a clear white flower with a golden centre collecting golden pollen. A beautiful light captivated the 'image' and scene. It was as if this bee was collecting 'life', 'love' and 'nourishment'.

The image disappeared to leave the light on its own which shoots upwards and upwards and outwards too. My mind with it. A second later, a bright green planet is covered in the light and gold flecks are sprinkled over it, surrounding it in a golden glow - 'the pollen of love'. A red planet appeared and the same thing happened again. Such peace. It was so beautiful.
(Picture Seventeen: 'A POLLINATION OF LOVE' page 124.)

I then found 'myself' completely tingling, vibrating in a sense and my normal 'senses' were returned. (N.B: THIS WAS NOT ASTRAL PROJECTION/PLANING). It truly was a wonderful feeling and so emotional for me too.

PICTURE SIXTEEN: A JOURNEY

PICTURE SEVENTEEN: POLLINATION OF LOVE

I hope and feel that everything here in these pictures reveals itself. The movement and the two 'bodies' of the beings with the use of their physical in their craft and as previously 'pictured', their body of light. Also their love and hope for us all. (Thank you so much for this experience.)

COMMUNICATION Contd.

Such beauty and love my son that we take and share with each and everyone of you and each and every type of 'being'. We carry light and move in light. David my son, we *are* light. Our physical 'selfs', our second bodies we do use but have used less and less over the last few thousand of your earth years. That is why you have only just caught a glimpse of part of me and the rest was light. (We are progressing too, as we have said before. . .)

Aha! David you have us in your mind, a name you have said a thousand times. . . (Pause). . . 'TRANSLEATIONS'!

As your tears flow you *do* understand 'what we are' and of what (in simplistic terms) we are about! Movement and light and of help and deliverance to open your hearts and souls of every 'Nation' and of every 'Globe'. We hear you asking to say something to us.

ME: Yes. As I sit here and feel you with me and at last *knowing* what I felt about you is the truth, my heart is overwhelmed. I feel so much more connected to you. If that is even more possible!

The feelings of love and peace that you bring, fills me with tears of joy and happiness that I cannot describe. You have affected my heart and my life and I just want you to know that I wish I could say more than 'thank you'. I cannot find the words that would tell you what I think and feel for you all.

COMMUNICATION: David, my son, my dear son. You do not need to say any words at all. We see and we hear and you say all the words that are ever possible in one single thing, a 'tear'. We do not need to say any more than that. We love you. We love you all, never forget that, please. (PAUSE)

Okay David, time to lift your heart and the pen's speed to fulfill the need. Here we go, *Deliberation* indeed.

As you gaze upon the clear night sky and see a hundred thousand stars or more in the blink of an eye, many eyes and voices say (and have said) . . . "Why?" Why indeed?

It is within us and you all to ponder a question. A thirst for the experience, the knowledge and the information that will lead you to deliberate at so much around you. Will the thirst be quenched or will darkness cover the eyes of millions?

As a sparkle of a 'star's' light captivates a mind with beauty. . . therein lays a mystery. Can these things be sought? Look into your past by delving deep into your history? Some clues have laid there and some still remain to be discovered. How soon depends upon the light's expansion and that lies with 'mankind's' apprehension and struggle to choose 'within' as a means of solving its problems and goals of unified peace and harmony.

As the lightening from the sky and the earth meet and a force is expelled upon and through a tree evaporating it's sap and disintegrating its structure - there lies another message for you. Nature cannot and will not ever be harnessed or controlled. It will fight back and destroy vast areas of your land if you do not live and try to be one together with all things. (Remember natural law).

The structure of evolution, the tropics, the forests, the mountains and the seas and its abundance of life destroyed by a bomb. Something that is going on and on right *now*. Will you see and will you heed? Will a crystal clear blue sea as once before be covered with death and decay? Please deliberate.

Cast those eyes and the search far and wide deep out to space and concentrate the search, your search to something that lies undiscovered. Not this time for a physical thing, a materialistic thing, but a discovery of a connection lost over 'time'. A connection to every race, a line of light and love.

It is this quest, this search, this deliberation that sustains growth in so many respects and has done so since your birth. It is your 'birthright', your personal and global discovery and goal. (PAUSE)

That's all for today now David as this requires us to spend some extra 'thought', so we will continue this when next the pen flows. Much more detail and information is to follow.

Always you are in our hearts and from the Great Spirit never to part. Be true, be you, live in peace. Goodbye from me and us and in love and truth we, the 'TRANSLEATIONS' place in you our continued trust. Love to you all. . .

ME: My love and goodbye my 'friends and family' to you, too. (Today was amazing, thank you!)

WEDNESDAY 1st NOVEMBER 1995 10.15 a.m.

ME: Praise be to the Great Spirit. Welcome to you all in love, light, truth, peace and harmony. I feel so warm and protected and know you are with me. Watching me and guiding me; a wonderful feeling indeed.

I pray for the light and truth to expand and encompass and to continue to nurture those in need and who are suffering on whatever plane of existence they may be. Every living thing to grow in the right way, every night and every day. Bless you all. Please let 'Deliberation' continue and the pen flow.

COMMUNICATION: We are here my son. Always and together in communication and love. The light will expand on its correct path to seek and to nurture as you say and so grow in the right way. Altogether and as 'one', it is not difficult and if many realised (and understood), it can be so much 'fun'. Not play of course, but a sense of accomplishment and progress and no 'ego', ever. People will see and people <u>will</u> grow (this will be so) we know. Let's proceed. . . Deliberation, consideration and to show.

Many avenues have been sought to satisfy an individual's quest for advancement and reaching out for the known and more importantly, the unknown. They consider facts and judgements to establish in their own minds in what they believe and what they don't to cast aside.

Directions in travel and of mystery to fulfill desires are inbuilt into them. To enrich their very being and their understanding of their own existence and of that what has created them and of that which is all around them. This is the same universally. Every 'being' and every race has considered and deliberated either <u>deliberately</u> for themselves or for others.

Many have simply thought and said, "What is out there?" Then have proceeded on to, "Let's see then" and so increased knowledge that way, to expand and comprehend. Others have sat down and in conference, known far more and wanted to know the 'how' and 'why', rather than just the 'what'?

Each is a different question, but the same answer will always arise to be shown to each and everyone and of every existence. Each line of thought, each direction travelled, each discovery made with whatever means are made available, will ultimately end (but not end) in the same way. A final acceptance of what, who and why they exist and for what purpose they serve in the overall 'web' of life.

Perhaps over the centuries this 'time' around, mankind is slightly different though. We see this and compare it to your previous histories of existence. It is different, your overall consciousness is different (by the way, it had to be!) to 'before'. Yes, a progress has been made, but nowhere near far enough - yet.

We see little things that many would not notice. Like an individual's acceptance to hatred and death or the compassion for others far more than in the past. We do not need to name names, but suffice to say that 'what makes one forgive another?' Wisdom, or an understanding of something more within?

Let us take an example of a beloved child who is killed, murdered or slaughtered. Such love lost and such pain. So much pain in bereavement that no counsel could ease your (or their) heart(s). And yet. . . the mother or father of that child says, "I forgive them,". . . for what he or she (or they) have done. How easy do you think that is to do; could you?

We are not saying that you are suddenly a martyr for heroism or for peace, but ask you to consider and deliberate on a wider scale of love and understanding of what *you* actually are and the part *you* play in the connection to the 'all', the 'Creator'. Please understand two things:

1) You cannot die and cease to exist. You are consciousness - soul, spirit and as we have said before, the body, your body is a shell. (Very important of course, as it enables you to *live* - on the Earth Plane - and learn.)

2) Secondly, because this is so, it does not necessarily mean that your eternity in 'love' is secured if you have not lived in the right way.

We are not your judge. Your destiny is of your own making and the outcome of your individual eternal future is down to forces that lie beyond, way, way, way beyond anything, that we cannot even comprehend.

Such words may seem to one person a helping hand, a guiding hand, but to another a whipping stick or lecture. As we've said you are your own judge and if we think in your terms, also your own 'jury'. Consider and be considered.

Let us go back for a moment to the example of the 'loss' in such a tragic circumstance. How can they forgive? Remember here. . . that they may forgive, but they can never forget - it is etched in their hearts. This is why love goes beyond the surface and the understanding of many at present but this will change.

'Love' is universal and it is eternal. It is whatever word you choose to describe. As we have said before, does one consider a love that has lasted a lifetime more stronger than the one that has lasted but for only the 'blink of an eye'? Love is love, it knows no bounds. This is why they can forgive (for) those that have suffered because they understand that love is not put in a pigeon hole or box or treat it half heartedly or with contempt . Do you follow what we are trying to let you feel?

We do not suddenly wish to be negative here, but we will cast our view on the persons or people who have not been considered to deliberate on *their* thoughts and actions and their ultimate consequences. Okay, they have inflicted pain, hurt and cruelty on a living thing or being. Make NO mistake, it is possible they may suffer far more than you can imagine, but here is another thought. It is very complex and may cause confusion and misunderstanding to those that have only just grasped the above.

There is, as you know, a 'Karma', a history for everyone of you. A 'slate' as it were and these can go back over many millennium since your first existence - your 'birth' of consciousness. We have said over and over again that life is for living and life is for loving. Now then, who is to say or for you to know, that the reason you have suffered so much pain is for *you* and *your* experience this 'time' around.

Maybe it was *you* that had to experience the loss, the illness, the disease, the hurt that is so acute inside you that you say 'I WANT TO DIE'. It is easy for us or for anyone not in that position to say, "We know you are suffering beyond anything that you can ever remember." But always know that someone, somewhere and somehow has experienced what you are going through and have considered beyond the normal comprehension of life, then turned within and 'understood'. This sounds easy and we know it is not during such pain because love is so strong and is so complex to you . . . , yet is also so simple.

People reading this may say "absolute rubbish" and we know that some will. We have also said that if one person, just one person can change and open up and give out their light then this book, this work, is worthwhile. Everyone is different and unique until the realisation of being 'one'. (PAUSE)

Those that have committed the crimes or acts of injustice should never feel 'safe' in what we have just said. They do not know and will never know that what they are about to do, or the pain they are about to inflict is 'Karmic' or not. An equalisation of the Karmic slate or an *unbalance* on their part which may never have another chance to be rectified.

As we have said, this is a very complex area, yet is also simplistic. All you can do is live your life to the best of your ability in peace and in love. However, that message is never an opt out clause or get away line. You are your individual destiny.

There is a question come to mind through you David and one that should not be ignored. Someone says, "I was forced to do that action," or "events were beyond my control." What if an individual is in this situation? Let us take a scenario of a hostage and his captors.

A man is told to kill - an 'order'. Does he feel less guilty because he was carrying out an order? You, the individual cannot ever get away with this blatant excuse, even if your life is in jeopardy from the 'power' held over you.

We would not also say that you should not ever defend yourself or your family against such an awful 'experience', but want you to know inside, that even in your darkest hour, you have nothing to fear. Ever. Hopefully, this will be of comfort to just one of you. Faith in love and love in faith, always.

You must therefore continue your search, your consideration of the what are you, how are you and why are you here? This will lead to your growth and the connection we are (and more importantly, maybe you are) seeking in you and your 'self'.

Well my son. Much for all to consider here and we know that what we have said could cause a lot of 'soul' searching. This is good, because then maybe you all will want to know more. Not just from us, but in the many other areas of knowledge and wisdom that many people have in their hearts and minds. Always strive for new wisdom and knowledge. It will come in many a variety of ways. Seek and you <u>will</u> find.

Goodbye from us in hope, truth and peace. Love to you all until the next time this flows. Bless you all too.

ME: Goodbye to you all till we 'write' again. You are in my thoughts and mind every day and in my heart. . . never to go away. David.

FRIDAY 3rd NOVEMBER 1995 10.40 a.m.

ME: My heart is open to you and to those of 'love' and 'truth'. Please let your peace and harmony flow through my mind and this pen, as always.

Light surrounds me and is within me to grow and to progress each day for others to share. Praise be to the Great Spirit and all of my family and friends.

My heart is here for you.

Is Deliberation concluded today and a new chapter to begin? My friends, the Transleations, you and I forever to be one. I feel you here with me now. . .

N.B: The candle flame was six, eight, ten inches high as the energy flowed through.

COMMUNICATION: The energy, the connection and the link to your 'physical self' is strong once again so the pen flows and we hope all of your minds do grow with the opening of your hearts.

Yes, today my son, the 'Deliberation' ends and Chapter Ten will begin so let us conclude on this particular aspect then.

"Welcome, welcome, welcome! Roll up, roll up, roll up!" A cry goes out at the fairground. Spend your money and make a choice, to take a chance. . . and win? Imagine yourself at a coconut shy and hear this cry. Do you have a go or walk straight by?

Simplistic is this scenario we make, and it emphasises many things to ask 'is anything at stake?' Is a coconut something that you would like to win, or is it taking part and the fun, the 'chance' that is so nice? Is it a gamble (or) with three throws a go, you cannot lose. . . and if you were to win, is it the prize that you seek? As we say, many questions from something so simplistic, but everything can be linked in the same way to the deliberation, or the debate.

Each of you are so different and so each of you look upon any scenario with different eyes, different feelings and consequently different actions. But the end result will always end up three ways. You win, you lose or it didn't matter because you took part anyway - to come back another day.

During this part of Deliberation, what we want you to think about is the feelings that you may have with this idea. Is it all fun and just light-heartedness what you see and learn here, or is it much more for you? Do you find it a joke, or a game, or does reading these things sound like all the 'same'? Yes, these are the feelings that can come to the surface, but it is the result and the direction you take afterwards that matters, that really, really matters.

A child may come to the coconut shy and have a go and cast his/her throw but misses and smiles to say, "May I have another chance, just another throw?" Keen to win and to take part - a thirst for wanting to please and to win. Would the parent let him or her. . . or walk away, "not now, maybe another day."

On a far more serious note, we say that opportunities come and go. We are not asking you to give 'money' for another 'go' but to acknowledge these openings to let yourself grow.

Consider so much more than that very second of that 'choice'. Go beyond it, open it up and seek.

One day you or your child may ask or say, "I feel this", or "I have experienced that". Do not discount it or push it to the back. Discuss it and nurture it. If you have opened your heart to something, do not then push it aside or into darkness again.

Many children on the 'Earth Plane' have many special 'gifts' that are waiting to be opened up. You the parent have the choice and can give them the chance, the opportunity to grow and to know. (Forget the financial aspect or angle - we do not mean that). Many will experience new things and feelings and emotions and will have so much knowledge and wisdom, that it amazes you. They are old 'souls' come to help you all. Love them, nurture them, care for them for they will help you all grow.

When a child asks for help and understanding and for another try, do not stare at him/her, but open *your* eyes. Look into the beyond and at whatever can be fulfilled. Look into love and nurture what is within and the beautiful stillness.

You may know of a son or daughter, nephew or a niece and amaze yourself at what and how they act. Are they three or thirty three? As their eyes gaze around, they look, they seek and know in their heart at what is to be given and what is to be found. They will consider and give themselves to all those who have lost their way - to help the generations to deliberate.

Are you the fairground, the stall keeper that controls the situation? Do you open your arms to those that have gathered, giving opportunities for those that have come to see and to try their luck? Is the 'goal' stuck on the pole, not to be dislodged or placed fairly for the ones that need to try to open up. (PAUSE)

Let us say for a minute, that you have gone and 'won' a coconut that you have taken home. It has come from a tree and been nurtured from seed, undertaking a long journey to come to thee. A food of wisdom in a sense, like 'light' and 'consciousness' that has emitted and given you birth.

THE SHELL

The shell is smashed and it contains food and drink,
is this, we hope, making you feel and think?
If you have considered and taken a chance,
you may win more than a spellbinding trance.

You can break open the outer shell, your barricade - that blocks out what is right.
To see what is inside of you, more than body - it 's love, and light.
A nourishment not all alone,
but once you've 'discovered', you're half way home.

What we finally explain is everything that you say and do are the things that make you wonder and consider what is the true you. Look and *feel*. Do not just watch and observe but grasp the opportunities. It is what is truth and is that of what you deserve.

Nothing hidden but a false confusion. It is your choice to find out if it is not an illusion. So whether you win or lose, or if by another chance, be true to yourself. No one to lead you in a merry dance.

A coconut shy, a lie to you all along - or a theory and the truth that will never prove wrong. Over to you to deliberate, debate and to consider. Then one day you will find out, your chance, your choice in whether to open up and to listen.

David, I know you feel the energy all around you as it sends the candle flame high with love. Such a high vibrational level for you to write and for you to tell. Take these messages of what we say so that people will understand something. . . one day.

Okay, Chapter Nine completed my son. Is Chapter Ten going to be full of 'fun'? It will be about 'growth' in and around your sun and your moon and how these have made many of you 'swoon'. Each galaxy has similar concepts and ideas and it is this that we bring you next time, to teach and to share. Many civilisations and many cultures are watching the night sky and crying out the 'how' and also the 'why'?

Till next time then, when the pen flows to write and learn about. . . 'WHAT THE HEAVENS KNOW'. Love, peace, truth and light, keep shining David - be bright. (for all to see.) We'll be with you always. Yes, that is true. . .

ME: Wonderful! Love to you all. Thank you from my heart.

CHAPTER TEN

'WHAT THE HEAVENS KNOW'

MONDAY 6th NOVEMBER 1995 10.40 a.m.

ME: Sometimes I do not know what to say other than you light my way and my day. I am here always for you, in truth and love and light.

Please know that my heart is here for you to continue. You may be so far way, but as I think and feel, you are even closer than yesterday, today or even my tomorrow. It does not matter which for in love and light we are together forever. Please continue with your Chapter Ten - 'What the Heavens Know'. . .

COMMUNICATION: Searching and yearning but always the connection is to be made or rather takes place. Two frequencies and two worlds are so far apart but *together*. Born the same way millions of years ago.

David it is funny how you mention the yesterday, today and tomorrow, for in the first part of this chapter we will show and hopefully enthral those that have lain in their sorrow.

We will depict and explain that you have so many similar traits on your world with those of so many others that hearts (we hope) can begin to see a stronger link with what has always sustained them. Those that have gazed into the 'beyond' and sought the answer to questions like, 'What is out there? What lies in the Heavens? What secrets do they possess and hold?' Yes indeed, 'What do the Heavens know?'

Today is part of a revelation of the past. A sort of uncovering of layers of both the inside or interior of the mind and also of what is beyond your planet.

From the beginning of your time when '*humankind*'. . . first gazed out along the horizon and could see what lay in front, above and all around, there was always the awe at the beauty and its captivation. There was something good that brought heat and light and something cool and mysterious along with millions of flecks of light.

Such mystery, such beauty, such magical properties that were always there after each cycle of the day. 'These were 'gods' weren't they? What part do they really play and what effect do they have on life and us?' they cried out.

Many civilisations worshiped and cried. Tears fell in hope that what they had offered to them pleased them enough for them to be protected. For the Sun to shine and crops to grow, the rain to fall from the sky, but always, always returning to the question. . . "Why?'

Throughout those times and 'ages', people concerned themselves with what physically sustained them - all part of 'humankind's' learning process. (N.B: We thought we had best change to this 'word' along with some of your recent thoughts David. We would never offend (or intend to) any part of your people, male or female. You are 'one' so words do not really mean a lot in that sense but for your feelings and thoughts we have altered it).

It is not uncommon that billions of worlds had or have first thought this way and it was natural. (As we have described before.) If something kept me alive then it must be powerful enough to be a 'god' - SUNGOD, MOONGOD. . . *No* gods of course! (But beautiful, so beautiful all the same when said and done.)

Many beings have had similar experiences with moons and stars that rotate around their planets and homes. Some so colourful and some so diverse you would say, 'these are unbelievable'. Each are connected in similar ways to your evolution patterns, giving life and sustaining life in a variety of ways.

There are SUNS that shine a brilliant black in an aura of gold and white, way out in a 'space' of dark blue in a dimension of space not known to you. Some planets of green and blue have SUNS of red and MOONS of golden rays of light, expelling different energies that help maintain the life of those that live there.

There is a place that we call the. . . how would, could you pronounce or describe this. . . let us see, you would call it a 'paradise'. We will not reveal the name of the species as yet because it is not right for us to do so.

What we can tell you is that life there for it's inhabitants is so peaceful, so wonderful and they live not with oceans and land, but of a substance of another kind. They move on layers and particles of light emitted from a star above them all at different directions and frequencies.

They can remain stationary or move by 'linking in' with these layers. There the 'sky' is one of a golden mist, but they can see through filters in their bodies. They also have an 'energy' of a different kind to your food. It is grown through spectrums of radiating pulses within the planet's 'core' emitting upwards through a surface layer of relays and communication points of light.

What we see there are colours that are so immense and diverse. Such beauty, such feeling of peace, yet for all this, they have and know of their goal of returning to the 'source' to the Creator. They have gone beyond what they have thought about their 'stars and moons' and gone forward in progress and to continue their education beyond normal thinking.

It is this initial concept of the 'yesterday' that every living being in different galaxies and the universe is trying to achieve with varying degrees of success. It is the 'beyond' that has *made* the planets, stars and moons and there lies the answer. That answer is not millions of light years away, but is *within* you. A journey but no journey. What made the planets has made you and vice versa. Nothing different, nothing extra, nothing more than love and light from the Creator. (PAUSE)

David, we listen to your thoughts as we said earlier and we are going to answer some of the many questions you may have, but at the 'end' of this book. We know that so many of you would like to know, 'How is this so? How was that made? Why was this planet here? Why do we have one sun and one moon?'

Everything will be revealed in its own time, my son. This is the same for every intelligence in this searching and reaching out for that something 'extra'. Know your feelings are no different now to when humankind and what you were before (that's interesting!) first saw the night sky and day and the beauty that they all contained. Here is a query, a question, in 'What the Heaven Knows'.

'I'm searching and ask where, why and how? Is there something else other than a burning sun and passing moon . . . are they two of a kind or more?'

Casting your eyes and hands wide apart and the opening of a heart signifies a lust and a thirst which has gone unquenched within the mind to search for an intelligence that remains. Forever in time across many galaxies lies the connection to you all and the beyond. Therefore what is found in the 'here and now' lies behind and in front of you eternally.

Gaze and see right through these words, what do you sense and feel? A universe that contains just you or maybe one or two?

There is such force and a power but in love and light these are the things that must be grown and nurtured to then set aside the outer mystery. For *inside* lies the answer to your life force and each 'Beings' eternity. (PAUSE)

David, time to go now. We do hope that you are not confused, but when the pen next flows you will understand more of why we have said the things we have said.

Love to you all in peace, light and harmony. Bless you all.

ME: Thank you. . . Love David.

TUESDAY 7th NOVEMBER 1995 10.40 a.m.

ME: Now I have had time to think, so keen am I to re-read and see what you say and show. Please continue and let this pen flow. Understanding and comprehension just two words of the past, to see through to the future. Bless you all and my friends and family - THE TRANSLEATIONS. (Pause.)

COMMUNICATION: We are with you and are so pleased with your pen to show the communication and for understanding to grow. Information and an explanation of the 'yesterday' and today is for the 'today'. We will explain this as we go.

As an astrologer points and marks his charts and watches for movement in the night sky, as the scientist calculates and tries to manipulate, change and search for growth in chemicals, nutrients and his machinery, there goes unnoticed what he is trying to discover - a mystery.

Much has been solved, but there is so far to go. Humankind's growth would (as said before) be so far ahead if just let to flow. Much searching and deliberation, yet not gathering and collaborating between the nations. 'Two heads are better than one' is said, so is the search going to end in dilemma, to wind up dead? This is a sad note to begin on but one of reality when not linked to finding the true goal. The 'inner' not 'outer' discovery.

From today there is a change of your collective mind - a linking of telepathy but still words of a kind. As each and one another spark in the direction of the light, there leads *your* discovery of your own insight.

The stars, the sun and the moons of many planets orbiting in every galaxy are now awaiting your enlightened ray of hope and of charity. An expansion, a creation that every single soul puts together in peace and in harmony, a justification of the knowledge and wisdom of the innermost love and devotion, the creation.

As you, the individual branches open and maps your own chart and destination, your destiny is the discovery of true life. The mystery is that each limb and each mind connects and intermingles, electrifying and satisfying the 'need', in crying out for true peace and intimacy. Souls Divine and misled in love - created together from the one above.

For today, much of what we will say will be in rhyme and reason. Follow the path as it is justified and can be used in any season. Winds of change carry these words across the pages and over the hand of truth to know that it is laid down in your hearts and in the minds 'eye' it <u>will</u> be seen.

As you see the sun rise and bring light onto the Earth 'plane', a dawn chorus of food and energy is given to all. The day is lit and you are wide awake, how much searching and knowing of the heavens do you take? Do you look and search and hold your head up high, do you live and cry or will you die?

The sun rests for another cycle or so *your* eyes believe, but it always continues, even though your eyes do not see. It 'sets' in oranges and reds and streaks of gold, keeping its secrets of those untold. Only because you may not have heard the voice of truth and light, do you think of the darkness of the night? And if you wait for a moment, is this the truth or a lie? Do you believe in fate, by asking why?

The moon shows it's cool and beautiful white glow, its space 'radiating' for emotions to flow. A pearl in jade did the Creator make, to light your way and to see 'who's' face? Such a mystery or is it really so, in these things that we speak of from a friend or foe. There is no mystery in your heart that fades, for the gap is one, that only *you* have made. (PAUSE)

Out 'there' is a force that could blow you all away, is this the truth, a true doomsday? No need to worry if you have wedged apart, the callings of the many, a true mind and true heart. So wedge open with love and hammer the door ajar so that others see truth *inside*, the shell . . . finally broken.

Many, many 'beings' are waiting for *you* and are not able to depart until *you* have seen the truth. Much depends on how you react to the open door of your heart to then gaze upon the eternal goal so that they can all see it won't be long to the interlocking of all 'souls'?

David, now imagine a star and a moon, a child's poem of the cow jumping over the silvery moon. You may not recall the words but link your mind with the picture of this and trace the light and wisdom from a face. Yes, a full moon tonight and you will see what we mean and so that you can grow in more ways to be seen.*

So much is out there beyond all of your todays and beyond what you earn and what you pay. Everything in its place we of course do know, but what are you prepared to pay to give yourself a chance to grow? Not a material price, but a sacrifice for yourself to be true, to get to know the *true* you.

The inside we spoke about of you and your mind makes you unique and special, yes humankind. Is that last word a human joke or is this 'kind' a different yolk.

An egg was born of love and light, just as the planets and stars of each sector were divided up in growth. Some were born millions of years before one another. This is how it was meant to be. To find *your* space, your growth and every beings *own* individual history.

The time is *now* to look forward not in reverse - to carry you all in a web of light - not a hearse. A rebirth if you like, of a different kind. Of wisdom, of truth that. . . is it in a church you will find?

Much conflict of opinions is here we think but this is okay because *is* this only *ink*? Your church, a place of worship is this a true home? It is of no molecular structure of concrete or a planet or a home in space. It is your very being, your inside, it's the one and only true place.

So you see, what the learning process of every civilisation has gone through and every 'being' and every race too was to unblock the mysteries and go *forward* in history.

These are the words that we wish to pass over, that the Heavens know what is *only* you. They contain every element that is in your *core*, nothing different but is there more? The Creator has given an extra structure to each individual until its time to soar. So fly and be free, to leave the today which really is your real tomorrow. Take flight my friends, my family. We have only tears of joy for you, not sorrow.

Those in truth and love will be safe, entering the inner boundaries to climb over every fence. The hurdle of your tomorrow will be seen for the heavens know the answers and you will understand what we mean. Sooner or later enter the door of light and be open to all the things that fly into your heart. Judge for yourself what you feel within - don't let others fool you or to make your choice that is yours alone . . . , a beautiful, wonderful thing. (PAUSE)

---

*That night tremendous pulses of energy came through me as I looked at, and 'opened' my mind and heart to the moon and its 'light'.

Well my son, time to go again and we love you all with all our hearts. Understanding the 'tomorrow' is our next part. Love, truth and peace from us and in 'God' the Creator, the Great Spirit we bless. Goodbye.

ME: Thank you so much (my friends and family.) Goodbye from me too.

FRIDAY 10th NOVEMBER 1995 11.10 a.m.

ME: I feel peace and calm and know you are here. Time to begin part three, Chapter Ten I hear. Bless you all my friends of light, you help me light the way and nurture me in my life.

COMMUNICATION: As your mind dances along with the musical notes my son, you find an affinity - a peace, a tranquillity. Such peace and goodwill in thy heart, oh my son, never to part. One of us and us of you, never feel lonely but part of the truth. Oh my son, your life is to lead, be one in truth and love indeed.

A humble servant and there is many of you, using life and its many traits to make and create the heart's 'rays of light'. The Creator gives back the seeds of life to you all to sow and grow as only you can. To trust, to live and to nurture so high to let your rays of love fill the sky. Over and over every mountain and every hill goes the beautiful 'still'. Let your hearts touch every corner of every land, lend your minds to give a helping hand. (PAUSE).

ME: What followed next seemed so strange. It is hard to describe but it was as if 'someone' else, something else was with the Transleations. Such incredible love and peace. As if this next part of the communication came 'direct' through a vibrational frequency (communication cord) 'alongside' them, but from where? It was as if direct from the Creator to me. Phew! How could this be possible? I mean, see what you think and where it was from!

COMMUNICATION: (Contd.) Justify your actions with love and peace to link your arms and cover the globe with an everlasting sea of gold. You are all the very core of what lies ahead and so much more, so be together the one and all. Listen 'inside' and follow the call, for if you are open and you are free, there is nothing ever that you need to fear, you do not even have to shed a tear.

Come to me the Creator's love, soft and gentle and soaring higher than a dove.

Look to the light and you shall find your truth, your pathway to knock on the door. Enter in and stand in joy and peace, it is everlasting just wait and see, there's much rejoice for you and thee. Always to remain in the heaven's flow and so much more for you to all know.

So let us keep on track and continue the circle of life in life everlasting. Swirling and spinning and where you end you'll never know, for the end is *never*, the Creator gives you eternal growth. (PAUSE)

Contemplation and a gaze far afield, a burning question from millions of hearts, "Why, oh why my friends do you depart?" But we never do, do we my son, my daughter and my child . . .

I watch over the many who mourn over loved ones lost or killed, and they look to the Heavens with their arms stretched wide - they seek and they cry, "Why, Father, Why? Why this pain, like a knife, piercing my heart? This aching, this aching, my love torn into two, never to see again and feeling so blue. . .

Then as I lie awake night after night, my mind in space I eagerly await a sign. A sign to make me understand why I have lost a friend, a lover, a wife (or husband) and a child's hand. What in Heaven's do I do now? Alone, but not alone am I. Am I?

I search this life and am now pondering the next, something that always took the back seat - not my time to take the test. The shadow has suddenly overtaken my world, my home, my very core of what life and love is all about. So now I will go into the field, the open space or the sea and shout - "NO! NO! Why this? Why this and these feelings that I suffer?" (PAUSE)

PEACE, be still and softly hear the whisper turn to a voice. Sssh, sssh, sssh, my child and children of light. You are never alone, never alone, never alone. You ache and you search yet I am here all along - inside - do you hear me now loud and clear?

You look and can look a million miles and beyond the stars, the planets, moons and auras that create a light and shine so bright, but I am here and there and always within. Look inside and touch my hand, I have led them to another land. They are safe, in peace and in my love always and forever, and you *will* see them again I promise you. Like a promise from the eternal heart that is all you are and can and will be.

Now, as you sit and lie on the grass, or floating on the sea or sitting on the edge with the wind's breeze touching your face, look no further, there is a trace. A spectrum of light from everything and every living thing. You may not see 'this' that connects all but it touches your Sun, your Moon and the planets near and far beyond. . . but you will, all in time.

The tear that is dropped upon your lips of pure innocence and of a cherished kiss, made you feel that it can never be replaced as it falls from your face. Yet there is a mood and thrilling peace that is drawing near as you begin to understand and I see your face with a slight smile from ear to ear. . . Then a crock of laughter as pure love and light drops into place to ease your inner fears.

A rhythm, a vibrational level that captures your imagination and mind capacitation, a grasping of the cord of life. Pull and pull and draw in on the strength - to leap over the shadow of death's fence. A rebirth in reality and a wonderful experience if you have lived in truth, peace and in love grown from a seed.

As a child hops and skips in the summer sunshine now, a feeling of freedom, beauty and elegance, an innocence so clear. Your arms raised up to the sound of an almighty cheer, "You are here, my Father, my Creator, my true God, my Great Spirit. I see your light in the blades of grass and the grains of sand, how did you make this beautiful land?" Then a question that so many have asked now comes from just one child, "How am I made, Father?" FROM LOVE MY CHILD, FROM MY LOVE. A simple or confusing answer? (PAUSE)

Many planets out there with burning questions and aching souls are waiting to realise your all 'one goal'. You are together, all of my children of light. So carry the torch of life and the beautiful everlasting light. Follow the cords of your heart and join together in one united 'Kingdom' of universal peace and return to the tree of life. Connect into the web. . . the web and circle. . . everlasting. (PAUSE)

ME: N.B. From here the communication seemed as it usually did, however with a *pulsing*, intensity 'within' me. . . a resonance so very hard to describe.

COMMUNICATION: Is all of this your tomorrow or your today, the tomorrow put off for another day? We have seen this said and done so many thousands and thousands of times, waiting and waiting till the right call, the right chime. "I'll wait till the resonance rings in my heart" - yet they do not realise that it is them that have to make the initial start.

It is up to you, the individual to strike this right chord, the right note and it is through tried and tested times that all will sustain and continue the growth. Tough times and emotions may flow, but you 'inside' will know that you are following a true path to take you to the door, but never feel that you have the last laugh. Each to their own and no forcing of opinions. It is down to you to fill the shoes and join the walk on the road of truth. For you to make the running and the journey your goal. To understand and to love all and your everlasting soul.

David, as you write you can see an image within your mind. Describe what it is please, we do not mind.

ME: Yes. It is a road and I see people like shadows. So many of them. The road is straight and there is a light - a most beautiful light of yellow, white and gold. The people are moving but I do not see their feet.

This feeling, I do not know how can I describe, or could ever describe it. A love so divine enveloping and carrying them forward? The light surrounds them like a guiding hand and some start to disappear because I cannot see. A man, a woman and children too, I see them 'all' go through and 'through'.

There seems no ending as I see, one by one, a silhouette, a movement towards the light and love. My mind is fading now, but I can still see the light, a speck 'glowing', as if it will always be. What a wonderful thing. Not sadness or despair, as if they never had any worries or cares. A love that lay before them and behind them, continuous and always. This was beautiful. Thank you from my heart. (Picture Eighteen: 'CROSSING OVER INTO THE LIGHT' page 145.)

COMMUNICATION: (Contd.) My son, what you have seen is a mass 'crossover' and you know that it is always endless, since time began. They do not walk or run and those 'behind' that you saw never ran as they did not or did not need to.

Let us say to you all, 'What do the Heavens know?' They can know nothing or they can know everything. (This will confuse some, but we do not mean to). The answer is this. It is for you to learn and for you to find out. The search is yours and you <u>will</u> find the answers. You will know them when you see and hear and feel them.

So, next time you feel all alone sitting on a hill or feel trapped or in despair beyond belief, search around and also within and feel and see what the Heavens know. Ask to feel the love and everything can and will be revealed to you all. When <u>you</u> know and when you are <u>ready</u> in your heart.

PICTURE EIGHTEEN: CROSSING OVER INTO THE LIGHT

Once you have found your true self and entered into the light, the 'beyond' past your stars and moon will no longer be the mystery. You will enter your tomorrow, your future history, just wait and see the truth will be. . . most definitely. (PAUSE)

Well David. Such emotion you have felt today and in your heart and mind. This is but a glimpse my son. Okay, time to move on to the next chapter - Eleven, but first. . . what would and will it be like to reside in another place of existence and in your words a 'HEAVEN'?

Many 'feelings' of many 'beings' have wanted to know and to 'wonder' of this in what lies beyond the 'grave'. Some say "we are all dust and we just disappear without trace!" Well, in Chapter Eleven, what we want to say is 'about' these things and what you will face and learn and how you actually exist and how others do too.

We are calling this chapter, 'LIVING IN A HEAVEN' - (Like a magical spell, a love divine, no Hell).

So till the next time my son, we hope you all grow in the right way. Yes, your yesterday, your today, your tomorrow always. Goodbye and trust in love, peace and harmony, light and us. Bless you all.

ME: As I look into the candle flame and feel love so immense, love and peace is with me - eternal. It is all so hard to describe what I feel inside.

Heavenly Father, the Creator, the Great Spirit - you are my light and my life that touches me, my heart and soul. (N.B: I then needed to try and write what I felt.)

'I am but a speck of consciousness - a speck of light, but am part of you that sustains all life. A flame of love and beauty beyond comprehension is shining down watching over me as my tears flow.

Father, dear Father, I now cry with joy. For life and freedom to say, to feel and to be. Of all the good things that there are. . . so beautiful, so kind and so wonderful to see. A Rainbow, a butterfly, a child on a mother's knee, protection, creation and a love so Divine flowing through the body and soul and all of our minds.

I have a thirst and you quench my very being. To know that you are here within me and in everything and every living thing. Thank you Father, for my life and soul, till I return, once I have fulfilled my goal.

Love to you, my family, friends and guides and teachers on every plane of existence that I have known, do know and will know. Always and forever. . . one together. David.'

CHAPTER ELEVEN

'LIVING IN A HEAVEN'

MONDAY 13th NOVEMBER 1995 6.05 p.m.

ME: I know that it does not matter that this is a different 'time' of day that I open my heart and soul and mind to your advice, wisdom and love. I feel a drawing in of peace and energy around and within me.

To my friends and family the Transleations, please let this pen flow so that people may know more of your 'works' and Chapter Eleven. Something so nice, so beautiful - the 'Living in a Heaven'. Love and light to you all. . .

COMMUNICATION: Please begin my son.

As you draw open the curtains of your bedroom window, the sun 'rises' and shines bringing light into your room and into your life. . . for a new day, no more sorrow. It pierces through the shadows of thy room and pushes open the areas of what cannot be seen or felt. . . or heard.

The mist clears on the frosty 'morn' and it fills your hearts with a freshness that some cannot describe, maybe they have hidden and found it too easy to hide.

As the light shines in, it is time to open the window before you. Push it open as far as it will go - close your eyes and *feel*. Feel your heart filled with life and the beauty. It is all around and within you and so is the hope and the glory of the stillness and everlasting love. A new beginning of the never ending story.

Maybe it is the truth of what the individual experiences or maybe it is false. Do you know yourself? Are you still in doubt? Do you read on or put this down to one side or back on someone else's shelf.

Much has boiled down to the opening up of 'SELF' and the very existence of what you and we all are and of every living thing. Now the 'time' today is to further this. Perhaps even put you into a spin. Not to turn and confuse your sense of direction or dull your mind, but to let you know that the overall

147

'destiny' is all one of a kind.

It is the intermittent place of existence and a much higher plane of vibration and energy. It is a beautiful place to be. A stepping stone for you and for 'all' and a challenge to further their future and *the* future history. It is called a *'Heaven'* by you and many alike. How? Why? What? and When? Many questions that you ask but too late if you are . . . dead?

Well, here is a bit of information and learning to take on board, (as said earlier), to put on a shelf or cupboard to store or to 'holla' out loud and feel ten feet tall!

Let us first perceive that you know nothing of the soul and it's journey and rebirth. Your body dies and you cannot understand 'that' of what is happening to you and your mind. You may state "Everything is so strange and a sort of mist clouds my vision. . . (here is a joke - am I Brahms and Liszt!!), but I've just died a moment ago!

How can I still think and see and hear. . . isn't this so very queer? What's this light that is but a speck, yet seems to be of a rhythmic state as if something is all around me. I know. . . I will take a closer look and see what happens. Maybe it is a kind of hell or is it 'Heaven'?"

As you drift now and feel it more intense it captivates your imagination. All this, is it still in time, a second passed or more? "Where am I?" is something that you may cry for fear of the unknown. . . (why?) "Am I in a state of shock? I know I 'am' for I think, I see and I feel. Where are the answers, please?

Further into the light I have gone and images are brighter now than the burning sun but not sore to my eyes and all alone am I here. . . am I the only one?" *Then you know*. (PAUSE)

ME: As this came through the candle flame was unbelievably ten inches high 'dancing' and glowing so beautifully.

COMMUNICATION: (Contd.) A voice, not heard but felt in the heart. One of such strength of love now signals and grasps your bewildered stance, leading you to a fairytale land of peace and love that is all around. You seem to drift but continue to know not where and then you sense another 'you' but you do not despair.

"Another 'me'? What is going on? Hey, it is not me that I see. . .", as if through frosted glass. You give it a wipe but not with a physical hand and then you see those back 'home', the same yet a very different and solid land. One that can be as close as though the holding of hands or touching of lips, yet as far as. . . infinity.

The glass is clean and the reality hits home and you see what I mean. There is your family that you thought you would never see, leaning over your 'physical' that is just 'remains'. Something important, it was your 'home', your shell, till the Creator weaved your return to the light, like a magic wand and a wonderful spell.

Tears of sadness you now feel so you shout and cry out but through the window of love. . . "do not cry!, do not cry!", to the ones you love and those all around. "I am here always and forever. Do not cry my friends, my family. I am here and so is my love". (PAUSE)

What is that you feel, a hand on your shoulder? Does it weigh heavy or as soft as a feather? 'Hello, my son. . . time to come home. Come and meet your family, your truth and the love that is there for you all. . .' Then you drift. . . and suddenly you are found in the middle of a gathering of feelings and truth and unity and you sense and feel others too. Your brothers, your sisters, your mother, father, your children, all part of your previous histories.

It is then and here that you know of all that has gone before and come to terms with your *new* freedom of learning and living in this unique way. To be an energy that needs no food of matter or feelings of despair. What's this we hear? - "Do I still grow hair?"

Everything is perfect here on this plane of yours. Your shape and size of light now taking the same form as you choose, or have chosen, but only to those that you need to show and be proven. (PAUSE)

There is a finite line that you need to remember and come to terms with. You are light and always have and always will be. Whatever form or energy pattern that can be taken or projected to others is nothing stranger than only that. It is not solid or of 'structure' but an image stretched for you to show, for you (and sometimes only for progress and for love) to see.

Let us move on and describe the passing over of those that *know* and have shown the way of truth and light. Not to continue in that realm of continuous learning but who will grow in another way. . . in the need to 'ascend' with the physical 'self' and structure too. To then create the light in another place to continue and develop the heart, the one of the human race, its souls and minds.

This is connected just as we have previously described but there is no shock and bewilderment. An immediate recognition of 'self' and the higher

'SELF'. There is nothing complicated in what we say or now describe. Everything is clear if you have nothing in your heart to hide.

Those that 'cross over' and know and feel the light enter your cord to a higher plane. Something to strive for and something for you to gain, not an 'ego', but a fulfilment of your life's desires and destiny. The time has drawn near and your physical heart, your pump, your engine has failed and ceased. Those that lay and stand all around you, try no more. They cannot re-attach your light to the cord. It has snapped forever, not to be reconnected, for what *is* different *they* cannot see.

Your body is there. . . but in truth it is not. They have the copy that is okay to be burnt or to rot. Your cord takes everything with you as your body is in perfect working order, one and all. What the Creator, the universal 'doctor' ordered and as an individual, you are unique to carry on to try to love and seek.

This time, you not only 'return' with feelings of what it was all like, but you live it. Yes you LIVE it, but not quite as you did before. This time not with blood running through your veins but golden *light* that carries, moves and sustains your very being. One that enables you to carry on a physical 'living'. This is what we call a higher existence. One for those that strive and continues it's true goal and one that is beginning to fill an empty 'Heaven's' hole.

A new place, a new home, for you all to join. For those that come together into each segment of the puzzle. . . a home that has no need to pretend, one that goes with those that 'ascend'. It is up to you all to strive to the goal and this is your goal alone as well. One that will enable you to be reached before the final 'wave'. (The fourth wave of Ascension we mentioned at the start of the book.) If you are not sure, trace back the steps. . . and re-look.

The first wave has already gone you see and the second wave is not to far to go. . . A few years perhaps. Only the Creator knows the exact 'time and date' that has been chosen by the light. Are you on the second wave? You will not know but in your 'Soul', you do. You *cannot* find out by any means for it is hidden until the day you pass over. It will also be the way that you have chosen. . . could it be in your sleep, or by the 'elements' with or without pain?

In all these things that we have said there poses questions that lead you on just like a thread. This is for you to continue to think and to feel and to learn so that you can become and also be 'one'. (PAUSE)

So far then, what we have described are the briefest of details. Ones of the immediate response of 'Living in a Heaven'. There is not a 'God' with pearly white gates and there is no darkness and hate to those of love and light. We know David of your thoughts just now. . . "What will happen to those others?"

Okay (briefly for today) we will finish on this as there is so much more to get through and so much more to describe of the 'Heaven' and the planes of existence, other life forces and 'beings' too.

Is there a 'hell' that the 'bad' people go? Not as such, many will be pleased to know. Got off lightly?. . . We think not for a soul in obscurity would be better to picture a hell than listening now to this of what we tell.

The light is always and everlasting. If a soul crosses over and is of such bad ways, where does it go. . . where will it stay? Listen good and listen close. Your soul's light will be faint and not be able to seek a higher level until it is ready. A wandering of infinite loneliness, striving for repent and forgiveness of something that *only* the Creator can wave forward and onward.

As said before, the Creator has never ever, ever interfered with human kind's future until these times ahead. It is still your destiny and you can and will succeed if you want to and *believe* you want to.

So a soul with an unknown length of 'time' to ponder, a hell indeed we ask you to wonder. A threat, a joke, a fit of laughter? Live your 'life' and we'll watch you fly not cry, but it is up to you to love not flounder when your time is ready to 'cross' over.

Time to go now David, and this chapter has only just begun! Much to tell you, 'boy' will it be fun. 'Living in a Heaven' are not just four words, but of what you will picture in your mind and feel in your heart. This will be so immense just you wait and see.

All of our love my son. Love, peace, be still and trust. All will be well with your situation in work and life. (A promise.) Be 'one' from our hearts to you, with a ray of light watching both day and by night. Always and forever.

ME: To describe the heat and energy that came all over me . . . Unbelievable, tremendous. Love to you all and the Great Spirit. My heart and light to you, feeling you. . . touching you too. Thank you from my heart, always. David.

WEDNESDAY 15th NOVEMBER 1995 9.30 a.m.

ME: I hope and pray that all of humankind and every living thing, sees, feels and touches the light and love. Such peace. . . such peace. I feel the energy lifting as I write these words, my thoughts and feelings always felt and heard.

Bless you all and praise to the Great White Spirit, our Creator. Please continue the work that you have set so that Chapter Eleven can continue with the love like casting out it's net. To capture. . . people's hearts and imaginations, from the youngest individual to the 'masses' of every nation. Please let the pen flow through your humble son and servant who wants the world to know.

COMMUNICATION: As you have looked upon and through the candle's flame to feel, to seek and learn you now know more just our name. The desire has never diminished has it my son. . . and it never will.

It is this striving forward and the thirst to accomplish more than what you think you are able to that really is in all of you, but so very often lies behind another's restrictive hold. Opportunities have gone and been sadly missed throughout history and in every galaxy there are thousands, if not millions of them since 'time' began.

Look again into the flame. . . 'ah ha!', did we not catch you out my son, or another lesson learned? This is a lesson that no one should forget. Did you inevitably look upon the candle's flame when we meant your heart's bright and true light *instead*. (PAUSE)

We know it is so easy to read or gaze upon literature or works of wisdom and knowledge and 'accept' straightaway, but few have progressed and learned this way.

It is time to look, think and listen with more than your eyes, your mind and your ears and dig deeper beyond those words, pictures and feelings that get you to open up and think beyond the. . . 'How weird' or 'How queer!' Each sentence, each paragraph, page or book is another opportunity to take a chance and to really 'look'. Understanding comes from deep within by touching *your* living flame and light thats growing inside to know you cannot then but win.

Therefore, when everyone is seeing with the flame of peace and love from the heart all will be connected, to be ready for their journey and spread their new wings of light to depart. Over and over again we say to learn these things so the real lesson can begin to live in another place and dimension. Almost the reality, of linking with a twin.

A connection, a knowing of like minds of other beings is part of the new goal. A linking and entwining of each and all kinds of 'souls'. To explain more of this 'Living in a Heaven' we are going to *jump* your mind's *perception* but to still keep it within your total comprehension of those that know and will know on entering their open heart's flame. (PAUSE)

The future is ahead. . . and the fourth wave ascended. A time in the near or far distance of your generation or the next that no one knows. The fourth wave has linked and connected to the first, second and third. Each has grown and nurtured the new plane of existence of your many souls and spirits new home and world. Now it can complete as it is meant to do by sending strands of energy to *all* beings in all galaxies with an implanted Creator's code of, 'I LOVE YOU'.

This 'time' the fragment, the energy and each pulse of the creation's strands will reach out and touch and hold every race, every being and every soul's heart and hand. In every corner of every place that can be imagined of the universe, these strands will reach to teach of what can be achieved by such love and everlasting peace. All this will be the 'centre' of 'life's existence' to be overseen by the light and energy given by the Creator.

The fourth wave is the FINAL piece of your destiny(ies) and it is said from what *we* have learned that it will be the end of the what, how and the why of your planet as you now know and perceive it.

What we have said may cause distress or panic but we hope that this is not the case. You are a 'soul' so you can never be destroyed. You can also never fail to exist. However, as we have mentioned many times before, there are many ways for the soul or spirit to continue and/or to last in an endless bewilderment. . . could this be your blackest hell?

Those that do not succeed on the fourth wave will still have their work to do because everything continues just like a life's cycle of the everything and every living thing. It will be the responsibility and feverish task to rebuild what is left. Then over the sands of time to perhaps rejoin. . . (which *will* happen) in another way or another form to the Creator's new home of light and love that will have been placed for 'all'.

What we are saying in another clear way is that you all have the chance to make this fourth and final wave, but it is up to you to identify and seek the true PATHWAY of your TRUE SELF from WITHIN. No favouritism or placing of an individual into any wave of ascension is deliberate as all ingredients and the necessary abilities of love are instilled in you all.

Each of you are different in looks, personalities and characters but inside everyone is born of light and love. How could this not be so if you have come from the Creator, the Great Spirit, God above?

For a short while we would like to retrace our steps for it is necessary to take you back to the link of the wave of ascension, to the living in another 'plane'. The new and true feelings of 'Living in a Heaven'.

Each future wave, the second, third and fourth has a special place or waiting point of pure energy that sustains all thats there until each individual has formed the gathering and correct number.

This is helped by a choosing of mass Karma to rejoin to the light. As each individual ascends and crosses over by day or by night into the beautiful light, they are helped and greeted by friends and energies of ascended 'masters'. Also with them are special (you are all special as we have mentioned before) teachers and guides that have come and gone throughout your previous histories and 'times' of evolution.

They help and nurture them all until it is appropriate for their true 'joined ascension' both in and on a wave of magical cords of energy and light. Each is linking into a twined beam that knows no boundaries of existence and speed to join the previous wave above.

People will ask "but what structure and infrastructure is everything contained?" The what and how and again the why! Valid questions and seeking out the answers, but there are also two things to this:

1) The answers to some things are that 'man' could not perceive and know until the experience itself.

2) Growth is like a child's brain. An answer can be given but can cause anguish and pain because he or she cannot understand or grasp what it is and it seems all pointless or otherwise in vain. Understanding, wisdom and knowledge is a process of the future and only in the future can all things be revealed. (Please know that the future is the truth . . . and that truth is the future.)

Too much power and too much wisdom has killed too many beings and many nations and worlds far too soon. . . to start afresh before they had to. A learning process that had gone wrong. Again, we say this is what has happened to/in your *Earth's* history - THREE TIMES BEFORE.

It is the future 'history' that lies hidden, but few indications remain on the land and in the sea. Where they reside is in your heart because no 'memory' of existence is ever erased there. It is Karmic and etched on your soul. It is only when you are in another place of existence that this can be tapped into and remembered.

Some of you retain special 'gifts' and who knows, maybe some things will be revealed before their time - or could it be the right time! Everything is revealed as the Creator defines in all personal growth.

David, you have a picture now thats in your mind. You can draw it if you like. . . though perhaps it will make it easier for someone if they picture it for themselves. (PAUSE)

ME: I will briefly describe this. Planet Earth is surrounded by a network of beautiful gold and yellow and white lines like a grid. There are four collecting points on it's face, each connecting and interfacing across the globe. Then each four parts connect to a massive brilliant light.

The light and energy given off is converging and joining to and from all galaxies in all directions. This being the new home and 'Heaven'. Beautiful! (Picture Nineteen: 'THE ASCENSION CONNECTION.' page 156) N.B: (I have tried to draw this but would like you - who reads this - to also envisage this for yourself as the Transleations have hinted).

COMMUNICATION: (Contd.) Okay, now we would like to tell you more of another world that is nearing it's time to unite to your new 'Heaven' with it's brilliant golden glow of love and light. (We briefly described this in an earlier communication.)

This species that lie in a neighbouring galaxy have progressed a little similar to yourselves. They have fortunately been able to grasp and unify the peace that is required to be able to ascend when the time is correct for them to do so. They are awaiting your light to be created and emitted so that they can feel and see the guiding 'hand' to carry them.

They have had wars, famine, drought and pain since their evolution began but through progress and the 'understanding' we mentioned earlier, have overcome these terrible pains of hardship and slaughter. Others see they are ready and their hand of love is bursting to branch out, but it is not for them to do so. They have to wait. . . for you. (PAUSE)

Is this pressure? Do you feel a responsibility? You must know that it all goes far beyond your front doorstep, your home, your street, your town, your city, your country and your world. This is UNIVERSAL. . . NOW! Humankind is to lead the way, a very privileged task we must say.

PICTURE NINETEEN: THE ASCENSION CONNECTION

These 'beings' have hearts now which are so true and the waiting makes them so blue. They ache and yearn to unite with you. It is their dream and we know that it will come true. They are called the (David, you must spell this how it sounds) AMARALYNES. Sounds weird? (This is your spelling of what their name is).

This stands for a crossing and meeting of their different paths and religions. A balancing of frequencies to a *level* 'plane' of wisdom and understanding. They are waiting and suspended at a crossroads for the correct 'fragment of time' and space when everything is in place. Nothing can be rushed through and they know this fact - obviously. They hope and pray for your destiny and your fate.

There is a thought that has entered your mind David. Yes, they have glimpsed and seen your state of progress too. Not all the lights that you have seen are fixed in the night sky as some travel and also seek and want to know the where, the when and the why? *Not* to land and be 'discovered' for it is not the way. Not tomorrow or today. Everything is mapped and in it's special place. So much ahead for all the human race.

It is time to go now David and we just want to say, "Please, please all of you. . ."

'HEAVEN AND THE PLANES'

Is this all true what we say and describe,
is this all true, a fact or plain lie?
Come on and grasp with your outstretched hand,
do you really think this is the only land?
Movement and energy and light's vibration,
a love that the Creator has beautifully given.
To every living thing that is in existence,
in every galaxy and on every world far in the distance.
There is a light that doesn't fade,
one that sustains both night and by day.
You will know and you will go to a special, special place,
yes, it is a Heaven, such a wondrous taste.
Of things to come,
and an experience for all.
To share in and live in -
the never ending goal.
The Creator has made this all to be possible,
so that every being can be closer to its presence.
Such a feeling of 'one' and such joy in that day,
it's the very best global and universal present we say.

Well my son, it is time to go till next time the pen flows. Love always and in peace and harmony and light surrounding you forever. Goodbye for now.

ME: Thank you to you all (my friends and family.) Love from my heart too.

FRIDAY 17th NOVEMBER 1995 5.25 p.m.

ME: So many vibrations and energy fluctuations are all around. I feel peace and at peace knowing you are closer to me, if that is more possible each time. My mind is expanding with your truth and wisdom and as I write I feel the pressure of your hand on my shoulder as if to acknowledge the love, the peace and the freedom thats with me now.

Please let this pen flow to carry on where you last left off. My heart races, yet also slows as if in rhythm of a ticking clock. Praise be to the Great Spirit. . .

COMMUNICATION: Please write again my son. As we see your love and your light shining upwards and outwards and glowing like a torch, a light, a burning sun, we are here as always. To begin and now go on.

As the flow continues and the rays beat out so far and wide, flowing upon every shore and riding every tide. Love, like an open ocean caressing and licking every stone and lifting those high enough to the light, where they can now see and grow each day and every night.

Swirling and swirling energy that is not contained or refrained from everlasting expansion. It has no boundaries and is infinite in every direction and every feeling. It knows all and is all. Everything contained but nothing can wane. Strength forever as we are all together, always remember this. As it is so, every living thing in their heart's core does know.

A Heaven, a passageway to everlasting peace but is your 'Heaven' any different to ours, is ours to yours? Of all the 'beings' in every galaxy in the universe 'they' are but the same. Only the perception is so diverse. All is the Creator and the Creator is all so Heaven is just a single word that describes a 'plane' of residence that we all wish to strive to progress to and beyond.

A hand of friendship is outstretched to all things that can grow and are of living substance. It does not matter what shape you are, or of what colour are your hair or eyes or whether you have lived a life of laughter or tears to have only cried. Truth and happiness and peace is with you no matter what . . . from *before* you are born and living in a cot, to way way past the day that you choose to physically die. It is there forever. It is true and it is justified.

Clear all of your mind for a short while and forget for a moment about your troubles and cares or of what tonight are you going to wear. Easier said than done, she/he says. Please do try, it is very important. (PAUSE)

Be still and empty your mind as we have said. Clear out the debris, the hate, the despair and hassle received today. Push to one side your opinions and beliefs and let yourself be connected to your heart and soul and in the light. As you read this it may be difficult to do. To much noise about or other things pressing you that are on your conscience. Pause and reflect for only five minutes at least. We ask you to be able. . . this moment to give. Please. . . (PAUSE)

"Okay, what is next? What am I waiting for?" I hear you say and think "Is the magical moment about to arrive, to make me understand or to prepare me in some way?"

Listen, listen my friend. . . listen. What do you hear?. . . Is it an inner or outer quietness and stillness that surrounds you? You need to *feel* not *hear*. Within this 'time' something may make you think. Is it a waste of time or do /did you taste the 'peace'. Did a dream come true? A chance given to know and understand the truth and the true you. Find a moment to see and 'see', we doubt you'll look back once you have tasted the sweet peace of thee.

Some have said that in the quietest room a thousand bells could chime and feelings familiar fall upon the sublime. Yet, and yet. . . a single person could raise his hand and say that in a fragment of the pure stillness of their heart there came a joining. A unique connection that enables their true 'self' to be acknowledged and to feel a part. 'A part' of what has given them life to grow and to know what is in the light.

In a way, here today we have come full circle. To want you to know the answer to the original question, 'What is it like to be living in a Heaven'? The answer is and has been and will be with you forever and has since you were first 'existing'. (PAUSE)

We have mentioned quite a few things in one or two chapters that can be said to run along similar lines of thought. Well, we now ask, "Do you remember your best, your favourite 'teacher' or communicator in your life?"

Trusted words? A caring smile and face to help you along and to give you strength and connection to make sure you make it through.

Often things were said and taught over and over again but because you wanted to learn and trusted them and knew the right things to say and do, you progressed and made it through. Well, we are doing the same here because as everything is from the heart, everything returns to the heart. It is from the heart that *you*, as an individual, will learn. (If you want to).

As mentioned, something followed in a way of duplication; well 'Living in a Heaven' is a line along this thought. Although you travel and will exist on another 'plane' and grow in another type of capacity, you are *already*. . . living in a Heaven! If you are confused then retrace a few steps and things may - we hope - become clearer.

Imagine you are standing by a pool of water on a beautiful summer's day. You see your reflection and it almost seems to reach out and touch you and say "Hey! I am you and you are me - two images and two me's. Are we really one of the same?"

The water, a life force upon your land, contains light and could distort your image if it should ripple and move. Is your reflection a perfect match or a twisted and forgotten thing of the past? Has a stone been cast and the image ruined and moved, not to return. . . but for a second. . . or tomorrow's lifetime? Think and learn, the clear message is here within it.

Some beings and many have disagreed and said or felt "What is this all about?" and rant and rave and cry and shout so we ask today, "What gives *you* life?" The air, the water, the sun and the earth and many things that combine to nurture and give you the chance to grow and to also serve. What is this then that we are trying to say? (PAUSE)

All these things are from the true light and energy created to SUSTAIN YOU. Take one away and you will no longer exist. Your 'bodies' crushed or twisted into a shallow grave with your soul to live forever from that day. What we are saying is that your Earth is a 'Heaven' of life and you are living in a Heaven created especially for you!

Unfortunately it is being savaged beyond all comprehension and this is why it is necessary to join together, the four Ascensions. A different Heaven again for progress and for growth for Universal unity, for peace and to go on living in another way.

So you see, living in a heaven is not resigned just for 'humankind' and it is not only just one of a kind. Heaven has a Universal meaning and exists on many different 'planes' of existence but all have and will forever be linked stronger than by a single 'name'. It is *by* the love and the light, that goes on to *sustain*.

All what we have just told you may blow away the myths of the Heaven, the Earth and the Hell. This is good we feel and we are not the first by any means to show or to tell. All those that can hold their hands up high and say "Yes, I've been blinkered," take off those dark glasses around your heart and your eyes, no longer the need to sit at the back or to hide.

Be open and look to fresh ways of living and of learning for they may take you on to many different crossroads to meet many different people who have words of wisdom and knowledge and truth to share. Be true to yourself, your 'self' and to others, all to care. (PAUSE)

At this time of your year the golden leaves fall from the tree. (Where you are David of course, not all around the world at the same time.) One by one, they're blown away by the wind. This cleansing process is for regrowth to carry on afresh and to live. To be made strong again at a later date. We ask, will you listen then go to learn or sit and wait? To regain strength that you *already* have.

The tree waits to see and feel the light and warmth once again but *you* do not have to wait like this. You are the light, the warmth and have every single ingredient that is required and so, so much more. Living in a Heaven can be four words to you or a change of your life or the way you *live* your life.

WORDS, JUST WORDS or a lighting of the new road and the pathway to carry on the name of 'humankind' and the millions of souls. Will the torch be bright so you can see where you place your feet, or blind you onto a beaten track?

We plead, we beg and give our love to you. We know all the answers are there for you. They are waiting to be found so you can march together onto the new but 'same' ground. These are the steps into light and the Creator's love. A love that you will know and will always grow. Give yourselves a chance, that is all we ask and could ask no more. The future of you all is yours to fulfill and the choices - individual. Will it still become something of a bitterest pill?

Well David, we have ended on a forthright note. We do not hope you 'see' as one of those who stand by, or 'gloat'. We have come and been asked to help you all along. It is all we can do because 'we all belong'. Always together and always one, could that turn out to be a lovely song?

Well we say again, time is drawing near and would you now believe Chapter Twelve is here! This is the last one my son of *this* book. It will be one that can be straight and to the point or mistaken or 'mistook'. What it will be will depend upon the bearer's heart and their hand.

Chapter Twelve will contain some answers and questions (that some of you may like to put together), but also a conclusion that is open ended like 'life' itself. Some things may be of a shock to some. This could well be the case, but to you all we say, be strong.

The chapter is of a simple title and is/could be of a little "Kiss 'n' Tell!" Sweet and innocent with a little bit of a twist, but one to teach and let you trust us. We have decided to call this one a single word. . . 'RESISTANCE!' Why? - All will be revealed.

Till next time my son, love, peace and truth and us. Goodbye and love to you all.

ME: Phew!. . . Thank you, my love and light to you always.

CHAPTER TWELVE

'RESISTANCE'

MONDAY 20th NOVEMBER 1995 10.30 a.m.

ME: There is so much to look forward to even though the last chapter of *this* book begins. I feel that certain questions will be able to be asked in part two of this chapter called 'Resistance'. So that the information and understanding will flow from them, for the people to know in their hearts.

Praise be to the 'Great Spirit', our 'God', our 'Creator' for the love and light that sustains us in whatever shape or form we have endured and lived. Please let the pen flow from the heart's centre and from my friends and family for there is so much to learn and to become. It fulfils our destinies along our separate pathways, yet they are also entwined. I love you. Bless you all.

COMMUNICATION: An existence my friends, my children, my family. One that is everlasting but in many dimensions, time frames and across numerous galaxies the path has been made 'rough'. A ragged and jagged road that holds and tempts the individual and masses into a resistance, to resist the truth, love and light.

Paths that have mostly been created by your own hands and your own loss of control in the very essence of your lives. To be led astray and often collapsing into the decay of futile hostilities and the objectiveness in hate and the spread of misunderstanding for those all around you.

Today we are going to let you know of a wide range of resistances that can be overcome or pushed aside. Some you will recognise that you have tried to run from and others by which you have tried to hide.

Following this, there will be some thoughts and feelings gathered across many of our journeys that we wish to share with you all. Perhaps things that you can understand and take with your own continued journeys and to your heart. Both of course are just the same.

Let us take a simple form of 'refusal'. An example of the nourishment in what you eat. From the earliest memory you may have as a child, came the time that you were asked or forced to try something new, something horrible or could it have tasted so true? The time when you were told "This is good for you. This will help you grow."

Some of you may have pushed it aside and hidden your face, "I do not like it (or want it), throw it away!" Maybe a parent or family friend said, "Do not worry. . . perhaps you could try it another day, or in another way?" Others *were* maybe forced and made to consume that which they hated or defined as 'bad' to then say, "I hate you!".

More than two sides to a simple tale like this. Do you learn to grow and know of what something is like? To try and to taste and refuse forever? Or do you resist even further and one day realise this was an opportunity, one that you missed.

We are all God's children in one form or another and it has always been said throughout history, 'respect your mother and father for they have matured and grown beyond your few years'. This could be true, but not always because of their 'ages'.

How many of you during your early growth, through your childhood and teenage years (and some beyond) have said, "I know everything of what there is and what it takes". A resistance of a parental structure or just a learning process? In one way right and the other wrong, to want to be of your own judgement and your own destiny?

Inside your heart lie boundaries of 'resistance' that you cannot define. Ones that enable you to grow (not always the right way), but also ones that construct and hold you in place. What we mean by this is that inside of you and your light 'within' is an automatic system that enables you to follow certain directions and causes, without you even realising it. One that also enables you not to develop or learn anymore than you are ready to (or are able to) without your mind and heart in unison and conviction.

Your pathways are each unique and individuals become what they each become because of some of these things that we say today. Is this fact or fantasy? You decide what you wish to take or if and what there is at stake.

Some would say then that you would and will only end up where you end up and in what direction you start off in life doesn't matter. Also, whatever barriers or walls of feelings you erect in front or around you will come tumbling down.

To a certain extent this is true, but because you are all so diverse in personalities and make up and one is sometimes easily susceptible to negative or dark outside influences that connect to the inner true you, deviation and resistance occurs.

It is the 'knowing' and the feeling of what lies ahead and all around you (from within yourself) that will enable you to punch and kick this away. (Not physically, but literally speaking.)

Let us go back and retrace our steps for a moment. Choices to make and directions to take. Outside influences and outer knowledge and what is *said* to be 'right' in every direction you seek and look and tread. Only if whatever is right for *you*, and it feels *true* to you, then it is right. We do not and never will decree however that someone should then (or now) become egotistic or above themselves and say, "I will do it my way!" or "I am going to do it this way and will not listen to anyone else". Of course this would not be right either.

What we wish to say is that when you take any new way of thinking on board, judge it for yourself and with your own heart. It is your life, your soul, your destiny and only you can overcome any resistance or distraction that lies on the outer or inner 'planes' of existence and in your own material world of living.

So, throughout time immemorial, those that have 'governed' by force and ruled to lead over those like they are the lowest form of life, had much and have much to be concerned about. They are misleading 'life' from the smallest child to the eldest of each community, to make them suffer in *their* greed and of their so low deeds.

We know that it has never been easy to retract and change from persecution and tyranny in any form and this has gone on in many places and far, away in other galaxies too. There are of course two problems to overcome here, one of which will not seem very fair to those that have suffered deep, deep pain both physically, mentally and the cutting in two of their love in their hearts. No matter what you are going through and no matter what is enforced upon the body and soul, how much did or do you resist? Is your resistance from the pain weak? Was it strong? Now, has it gone?

Words that we say are very easy and when not in the position of what we describe, people will say, "Huh, what are they talking about?" Or/and, "Don't they know that we still have some pride!"

Please listen and listen with only your hearts. Every person has a choice in every sense, in every situation, in every conflict and every problem *you* may find yourself in or of those around you. You can say NO. You can say "No, I will not condone what you are doing or what you are saying or making us do". You can turn the resistance *outwards* to face that which is tearing you or your family or your world apart.

We know that every single one of you has the capability and the love and the light that is your very existence. To be in peace and harmony and not be forced to believe in something or to do or to act in a way that deep inside is not *your* way.

We are not saying that a single person should turn to 'arms' but to decide what is right for you. You do not have to be led in any way, or pulled in any direction other than what is inside your heart's flame. "But, but what of the consequences?" we hear so many (and have heard so many) cry out aloud. 'What are they, these consequences?' We ask in return. A loss, materialistic(?) Or of something or someone you love? There is no greater sacrifice than love that you can give to another living thing. It is a most beautiful thing when there are other easier options open to your heart and mind.

Always remember you are Spirit and you are a soul. Your body will die but you will always live on. You will go on to learn more, to go on and to live 'physically' again or join the light ahead and of course 'ascend'. (PAUSE)

Imagine for a moment your husband, your wife, your child in a perilous situation. One that is not a nice one to even contemplate or even debate, but we feel that perhaps you'll understand and know it is justified.

A happy family then and they are all together hand in hand. The ground opens up before them and a loved one slips over the edge and you(?) are not the one, who is clinging to the ledge. What would you do? Perhaps you would reply . . . 'Thank goodness I would not have to take part in this awful scenario, this plot. . . this play'.

The love that holds on to their hand is a driving force that nothing could break, a love divine that only you could possibly know. The look that you hold into each other's eyes, is it your beautiful wife, (or your 'rock' that you base your life around) or is it the innocence that defies all the scriptures. Whose life now flashes before you and is it a still or cloudy picture?

The pain is too much and you cannot hold on, "NO, NO. . . my love, please, please hang on." Then as your fingers slip and their eyes begin to drift and fade into an empty space, the darkness and the shade. A scream then erupts from your heart like a volcano. One that rips open the cord of your life's force and direction with the 'no' and the 'why'? It should have been I. It should have been I to have fallen!. . . "

On the ground you remain curled up like a ball and a fist hits out. . . but of course in vain. You want to resist and stay in this place forever. Somewhere that could seem to be close or closer than the never, never. A physical hand now comes to your aid and your side. Somone to take you back to your family home.

There you both cry and the tears run deep, never to cease both by day and night as you sleep? They *will* go away please trust us we say, but your love, your immense love will forever stay. At this time you resist again and your heart's resistance builds a tougher and stronger barricade than it has ever built. No light could enter this tunnel - my new home to live and dwell, 'Is this truly a living hell?'

We would like to say that in every loss of your love, in your heart it *will* always remain and will go on and be stronger than that day. In your darkest hour, drop your barriers of the black and hear the whisper and the calling of the light.

Yet in the tunnel you will find there a speck of light and you will go to it with your outstretched hand once again. You will join together and there will never be any blame. As your hand and their's reunite in a spark of beautiful golden light, it is a connection of the truth and the beauty within your very essence and your soul's creation.

Together, forever, no one can ever defy for nothing will stop love . . . there is only a parting of 'time'. A day, a week, a year, a lifetime? Ten generations? Only your soul and the Creator knows the answer.

What we are hoping is that you open up to hear and whether you have been in any situation of loss, hold no bitterness, resentment, hate or despair. A resistance of 'blindness' that can cover your eyes will, in the end, be swept aside. We hope that you can open yourself and push this aside so that you can *grow* and *see for yourself* and not rely on what ANY SOURCE ON THIS PLANET OR ANYWHERE ELSE for that matter, states, decrees or makes you fall on your knees. (PAUSE)

There is a beautiful light, it is called the Creator so please turn to the love that is *given* to you all then you can and never will look behind you. Your pathway can be set and all you can do is to do *your* best. No one to say 'you never tried, you never cared' or 'you couldn't give a damn'. None of this 'wham, bam, thank you mam!'

Think of every living thing and treat it with the respect and the care you would give to yourself. All join together and you will *all* succeed, never to sink into the depths or to plead.

There always has and always will be the resistance and its part to play. To delay, to sidetrack and to force you to be led astray. Find the strength and push forward with your love and everything will crumble just as we have said. Learn to live and live to learn, be one and be still. . . to become.

Time to go now my son, and the first part of this chapter is done. Prepare some questions and we will try to answer them for you to understand and grow in 'love'. Questions from your heart and your mind will come and they will help many to go from here and go on. . .

Bless you all in love, peace and in truth. Till the next time the pen flows. Goodbye.

ME: Thankyou from inside me. My love to you all. You have so much love it touches my very heart and soul. Bless you, too.

(N.B: The candle flame was incredible. The energy I could feel around me was sending it eight to ten inches high, but also the base of the flame was wider that the candle itself! - As if energy was pulling it in all directions at the same time!)

FRIDAY 24th NOVEMBER 1995 10.35 a.m.

ME: I hope today that you can help us in our future goal to love and light. If you are able to (or allowed to) please answer just a few or more of 'our' mysteries and unanswered pleas from our hearts. In love and light and our search for what we do not know. Please let this pen flow and to help us grow. My love forever always to touch your heart.

(N.B: I also needed to say some private 'prayers' here and it was after this and the feelings of such incredible love flowing 'through' that I broke down. It was so spontaneous as if a 'connection', a 'oneness' so simple yet so hard for me to describe to you. I would have to say that during these times, they are the happiest of my life. . . as my tears flowed. . .)

COMMUNICATION: We are here my son and have been waiting since we last let this pen flow for you to adapt and to prepare what is or has been in your heart and mind. We knew and understood what you would like to know, to progress and to also share with others.

Please remember that we are here to guide you and all those that wish to be helped to inner growth and contentment of the inner discovery of truth and love and light. It has never been a desire or inclination to try to change or alter your destinies by what you could call your 'exterior knowledge' as you *can* change your destinies only from within.

All of this is very complex of course because many would say that just by us communicating, "*you have* changed it". This is true also, but so far throughout this 'work' together we have not given or taken or diversed information that could be deemed as altering your future(s). . . other than to try to change the way you think, feel and interpret what is already in your heart and all around you. . . yourself.

After all, you know the answers to every question on a soul level. It is understanding this and being able to link with your higher and truer 'self' that all knowledge, wisdom and understanding will (and does) come from. It is the barrier and resistance to this and the exterior forces and feelings of what this chapter is all about.

We know of your questions and your answers you seek. Do not worry. . . we will take each of them in turn and give you what is necessary to know and to grow as you *yourself* have just said. (PAUSE)

Remember what we decided recently in chapters ten and eleven. Let us take you back to the teacher/pupil scenario. Again you can find an example. . . at school or college or even in this, the school of life and growth? If you know the answer, the structure or the contents of the exam or the test, what would be the point in taking it? Little or none?

If you had already determined the outcome of any difficulty there would be no point in the 'taking part' would there? Could it also be linked to a simple game of any sort? Remember an adult or friend telling you, "It is not the winning but the fun together in playing the game, the taking part that counts!"

David, it is the same with all life. Your life, others' lives and every being that can breathe and is of the truth, love and light. 'Life', we have said many times before, is for learning and living. Life is for living and giving, life is life, life is you . . . you are life.

Life is for love and for sending it from your heart so that it can help nurture and give a helping hand to a fellow friend or the person, the animal, the insect, the plant and the very core what is in everything . . . light and love.

Everything is so easy yet made so difficult by those that resist and twist and turn to boundaries and restrictions of the darkness, greed and destruction. So you see my son, what we can give you and what those that help in many similar ways is very delicately balanced. What we are able to give to you all are indications and probabilities and guidelines. We have not and never will be your only answer or only goal for direction or be your (and 'humankind's') judge and jury.

We know and understand that this work that is being done through this 'pen' will have an effect on many and we hope that they can progress. Remember though, that it will be the *individual* that chooses to alter or change themselves and not just by words and pictures on paper.

It is the individual who alters, changes and punches a way through their mind and heart's darkness to grasp the light with an open hand. It is they who will put feelings and thoughts to what we have given not us, because it is all within each of you. You are both independent of one another yet all connected.

A hope that lies 'within' will cast out the resistance and any blocks of hate or sin. By doing this, (and the connection of the self) you will then inter-connect with others and force the light and frequency of vibration within and all around you to break free from any shackles that tie your feet, your hands, your hearts and minds down. (PAUSE)

You remind us all of a closed flower bud or the newborn wings of a beautiful white dove. As the raindrops fall on the flower bud and the rays of the Sun makes it grow, it begins to open up and let it's beauty show. The rain, the love of the Great White Spirit touches its very centre and quenches its thirst right through its very existence and through its stem, its core of life. The Sun's rays sustain it and it remains open to the light to flourish and to let all who wish to see the wonder and splendour. . . 'see'. (PAUSE)

Oh yes, you all are like flowers to us you see. We want you to all open up and let your arms, the petals of your very heart open wide to let the essence of what you *are* rain and shine for all others to see and to feel.

Once you have acknowledged and understood, you will then know that you each are free, to take flight over land and sea and to go wherever you wish to go. You are the dove ready to fly high and wide to grow. Each of you are the birds of peace. The birds of paradise which have the strength in your wings to know, grow and to fly to where you belong which is in your hearts and in your souls. The strength will depend on your own conviction, your own direction to the light, away from the darkness.

What will feed you? You will need to seek and now learn. The works of a book, a film, a picture or the rays of light from the Sun or Moon. Everyone of you can and will be so very different and will look to grow and feather your own nest and your lives of love and light in so many ways that are just too many to mention.

Each will know what is right for you. It is and has been said that there are as many 'pathways' as there are souls. Life and love are infinite. They have no boundaries. Only those that you place on yourself and those around you.

You are your own destiny's influence and *you can* open like the flower bud and *you can* take flight to the everlasting light and love. You have everything within you. Everything that you could ever possibly ask or want. You can touch, feel, see, think, caress and love and grow with it. Push any distractions out of the way with all that is in your heart and you will succeed. Yes, a promise, yes indeed. (PAUSE)

Time to move on my son and time for 'growth' in what you seek and learn. What we are about to say you can all take to your hearts, or throw over your shoulder like a pinch of salt. To throw away or a wish for good luck? The decisions are yours to make and the information to cast away or to take.

Now let us begin with your questions and list. . . time to 'kiss and tell' of fate, with a little twist?

ME: Thank you from my heart. Here are my questions....

Q1. I think the first thing that many would like to know of is a little more about you. How old you are? What your lives are like? How do you live? Do you 'physically' die too? Also, more information on your home and travel would be nice.

COMMUNICATION: Here we would say to you David, that we were born and then grew just like all of you. From the seeds of light, love and *energy*. We evolved with different needs and of different tastes, requiring a 'food' of light and it's energies too. We do not eat by a fork or knife but infuse or digest the *rays* of *life*. We have a very different 'frequency' to any other and this is also what enables us to live.

Our species (if you like) were born at a similar 'time' to your Sun that exists in a very different galaxy to yours and of one that there is only *one*. We do not 'age' like your physical bodies, but evolve over a long period of 'our' time to link with a greater consciousness. A sort of linking of a greater 'mind'.

We described earlier that we are also of light and at the correct time for each of us (as an individual progresses) we return to the higher frequency. Which in a way is not too dissimilar to your soul's progression is it not? Remember no life, not a soul or Spirit can ever die but lives on a different 'plane', a different dimension and frequency and a different way of existence.

171

Our lives are dedicated to yours and other's progress. We do not tire or divert to anything else. This is a most rewarding job. Our recreation, our very existence is to love and nurture others. You could say, we love our 'work'! (PAUSE)

Our home is beautiful and consists of such a diverse atmosphere that can be only lived upon by us. We do not breathe air or gasses or chemicals. We are light and live, feed and grow with it. Our physical bodies we could say, can really be an illusion but still necessary to project to other worlds and places. Some could, or might say that if they could not/cannot see us, then we are not 'real'. . . part of *their* growth and understanding, we feel.

Q2. You mentioned that your 'home' is one thousand light years away from us and that I would need to see with fresh and different eyes*. Do you mean a special telescope? Also then, are 'light' years how *you* would also interpret distance and time? (N.B: Part of the answer to this question came in the answer of question three.)

COMMUNICATION: Yes indeed, one thousand 'light' years away. A distance that you said that you could not imagine. It is nothing for us. Nothing at all, this distance in time and light.

Time is a dimension that only some of you can perceive in other ways at this point. One day you will all learn what 'time' is really an 'expression' of. Suffice to say that time exists but it does not in the way that *you* only perceive it.

The Stars that you see are only but a few. You will need to develop far beyond your capabilities to see the *magnitude* of what is really out there. To answer one of your questions, 'light' years could be described as a 'Universal' link - (but of course in other expressions, ways and words) - of distance and if you like. . . time.

Q3. To help me see your twin 'home' you explained, 'to look beyond the smallest Star of this constellation'** and slightly to the right, you will see the flicker of light - our home'. Is the smallest named (what we on earth call) MEGREZ?

---

*A reference to Chapter One.
**The Plough, the Big Dipper, the Great Bear.

COMMUNICATION: Read the words and look again my son. Are the different eyes a telescope or the eyes of your heart's flame? Look beyond the Star you said you call 'Megrez' and open your heart. . . and you will see. No more to say on this as you know the answer within.

Q4. (N.B: I would like to ask some questions about planets, moons and Stars. . .). It has been approximated that there are some two hundred thousand million or more Stars and 'Dark' Stars in the Universe. Is this an accurate sort of figure? Wouldn't we need equipment far greater than we have available at the moment? (Max 23rd Magnitude* with the longest photographic exposure to see these.)

COMMUNICATION: We see what you have written and we just have to giggle. . . but not to poke fun. Is the figure you mentioned a learned guess or a figure that someone has plucked from thin air? Multiply the figure by one hundred thousand times for an answer that every scientist/scholar or astrologer would say, "Can't be - this blows my mind."

The problem that you cannot see is that you are still thinking in a 'time and space', you need to branch out your minds and let them take chase. The Universe holds many keys and many mysteries. . . there are passages of 'time and space' that cannot be imagined or revealed for the Stars lay hidden too much in someone's mind and perception.

The Universe is a magical place indeed. A Creator's gift containing life and light in every degree and decree. Beautiful, amazing. . . no words could ever say.

Q5. Much mystery has surrounded our 'Moon'. Scientists have established it's age between 4 and 4.6 billion years old and older than the Earth. How and why did it become to be in such an irregular orbital position? Also, what (if any) purpose did or does it serve? Has life ever existed there and why does it capture our imagination so?

COMMUNICATION: We like this one. . . and acknowledge the mystery and its captivation, a beautiful sight in a clear night sky when its 'full' like a magic pearl or eye.

---

*The term used in astronomy to designate the apparent brightness of a star as viewed from the earth.

Your scientists have estimated well, but know nothing of it's origin or purpose. Your nations wanted to know more about it and found the capability to do so, but will not find it's history in the 'dust'. It's *life core* faded away many, many years ago, before your existences.

The moon does not exist as it did then. Before, it was a living home for some that *roamed* travellers that needed a resting place far from their own galaxy. All we are prepared to say is that it came to be where it is now because it was necessary for *your* growth and your capabilities that would expand in time. (As well as influencing much on your planet.)

Also if it were not there, could you have ever contemplated progressing further to your nearest planet. The moon was caterpaulted with such force from a Supernova that took it's life force away, an event to lie on the fate of those travellers. Their destiny. . . and now your beautiful moon. (No more can be said at this time on this other than 'life' exists everywhere... but not as you often perceive it.)

Q6. Why have certain 'Moons' like those around Jupiter and Venus, disappeared? Example - Vulcan which was observed for one hundred years and has not been seen since 1876.

COMMUNICATION: We answer this with a question to repeat to you to think and open up to a new way of thought. "Who said that they were moons?"

Q7. (N.B: Regarding UFO's and so called abductions). You mentioned that 'full' appearances of any kind - Space ships, etc., have not been made - (due to fear) but why do so many people claim to have seen, witnessed certain events or experienced 'phenomenon' linked to UFO's? Also, are there really abductors and if so why? For what purpose does this serve to those that experience this and for 'those' who 'abduct'?

COMMUNICATION: Mmm. . . interesting my son. Intriguing, to catch us out? We laugh, not shout. (PAUSE)

Throughout your history and modern times, much has been seen from your hearts and the night sky. Much that can be seen could be explained away. . . but for these sceptics we now say. You have been watched and you have been studied too, but the truth is here. No harm will ever, ever come to you. The fear factor will remain till the day is right, a never, a maybe, or possibly one night.

174

The abductors and the experiences you mention come from a life-form from another place - another globe, another nation. Many claim that they have been operated upon and even have the scars or mental feelings from them. We are not a judge - everything is linked and it does happen - *but* nowhere near the degree of what you are saying. We know of but a handful only and all other knowledge is learned from the group consciousness 'mind'. Not to deceive or to make you feel blind but for those to open up and to try to understand.

What we can guarantee is that whatever anguish and fear you or anyone will ever feel is in the destiny of the individual. However emotional you may feel, you can never be hurt and die. The Creator will never allow that. 'He' is the Abductor's guide and yours too. Never be afraid, but for us of course, it is easy to say. We know this.

Here is a return thought and questions. If you could be taken away, you would learn from it yourself. (i.e. Through the actual experience although you would think it was against your free will. Or is it?).

a)   Why did you not die? (If they can do these things to you, they could quite easily make it so).

b)   Is it your's, or their destiny to participate and go through with it?

Q8. (Re Mysteries.) Regarding Crop Circles, so much interest has been caused by these. Are they false, hoaxes? Or if they are a communication, who are they from? How are they made? What do they stand for?

COMMUNICATION: Mmm okay. Many hoaxes and false descriptions too, however some we can say are a *real* message for you. They are created by energies given off by a group of 'beings' called the GALLENTIALITS.

They travel the galaxies to help with progress for you, 'humankind' and many others. (Remember, we are all connected). These energy *pulses* that are sent down (and also upwards) through your Earth's 'electrical' connections with theirs cause the patterns and sometimes beautiful images to be created. You will never know their 'real' identities, or see them. (SORRY). Only the connection will be given and remain to be viewed.

In time there will be a Soul 'reborn' to the 'physical' plane, (whose son or daughter?) He/she will have an uncanny way of deciphering them. Until that time, those that study them should continue to collate information because their job is important for that 'special' person to come.

175

Q9. About Stonehenge. . . Who constructed this and other fascinating sites of mystery? Was it visitors of other worlds? What was/is it's purpose? What 'energy' and energies were used or generated and if at all do they exist still today?

COMMUNICATION: Stonehenge did not suddenly turn up overnight and neither did any other site of 'mystery'. They were built with human hands but *were* given a helping hand through the light of their day.

Records of a written kind and of the mind have been lost or destroyed forever. The helping hand came from many sources and influences of energies that were sent to nurture human growth. Many rituals are performed on many sites because the energy that is/are in all of you still 'connects' there. You are all part of the Universal energy and light that is within you on the path you walk on and all around you. (PAUSE)

Q10. Re 'Science'. Will any cures for diseases, such as some form of Cancers and Aids be found?

COMMUNICATION: My son, this is down to *man's* progress. If we were to tell you the answers to these, would it not burden the hearts of loved ones if they knew the answers or would it give light to others? This one is your growth, your future history and your destinies.

What we can say is that these diseases and 'killers' have all been around for *centuries* and *centuries*. They are not new. The names may alter and change but illness and decay stems from the darkness within and around you. Different 'forms' but they are all the same. (PAUSE)

David, we know that you now have to go. Your life is busy and you need to work. Thank you from our hearts to listen this way. We can continue tomorrow where we left off today to finish this part my son. Do not worry, we are always here to stay.

Love and light and peace and truth. Goodbye.

ME: Love and goodbye to you too from my heart. Thank you.

SATURDAY 25th NOVEMBER 1995 2.00 p.m.

ME: (N.B: After a prayer) - As requested and desired, please may we continue with Chapter Twelve, part two, where we left off. Bless you all for your 'time' and your love and light.

COMMUNICATION: As you see the beautiful light's flame of the candle and of your heart David, we are here for you as we have said. We know of your past few days and wish to say to you, carry on as you have been with the trust in your heart. You will see that your private hopes and wishes will materialise and the happiness for your 'family' will be so. Always know that there is love all around you. So much love and you must share it, bathe in it, bask in it and give it to others who are in need.

We have seen many tears, wipe them away with your heart and we promise things will be okay. 'Trust' my son and trust in yourself and those around you. We understand your feelings and feel for you too, you are part of us and we are - as we have said many times - always part of you. (PAUSE)

Okay, now your head, heart and mind to be lifted up high to re-begin this part where we left off. Before we do, we want to mention that our reply will not be to everyones satisfaction and we know this. There will be chastising and condemning but there will also be an uplift of some hearts and souls and minds. This will always be so until those that doubt and cast their old 'selfs' to one side and turn and open to the light and peace and harmony.

Many will not understand or even listen until they have physical evidence before their eyes. We would say to them, 'You condemn those that have witnessed events and have had enlightened experiences as paranoid, liars and sometimes freaks and you cannot accept the 'irrational or rational'. . .' Even though in your life you have looked and gazed upon something or someone and discounted it, (or them), only to find that it was real or a long forgotten friend. A mistake or misapprehension on *your* part.

Those that have experienced this simple mistake of recognition need to face up to the fact that what is revealed is not always fate. Even when something has been proved verbally or been sighted, it is still beyond them and is then discounted. Closed minds and closed eyes, ears and hearts. One day the realisation will split them literally in half in knowing that truth will open their outer shell to reveal the light. One day. . . one day. (PAUSE)

That was something we just had to say. Now let us move onto your question of 'history'.

Q11. Re History. You had described earlier that humankind had got/arrived to this stage of existence/evolution or life three times before. Can you tell us more information. . . for example, the when, who and what was the relevant causes of destruction?

COMMUNICATION: Okay, earlier we stated that this is the chance to ascend, to no longer pretend. Over the millennium, 'humankind' had been to this stage of knowledge and wisdom three times before.

It has been three things that have led to destruction and the light to start all over again and to rebuild and to re-nurture. These events were entirely different in the way they started but the consequences and the end were the same. Total devastation and pain. A cry out loud from millions of hearts returning to the light. Such force, such pain before the realisation of what they were, not simply nations divided in a global shame.

The first event of what we describe came from the fiercest of *wars* that escalated beyond anything you could perceive. David, your mind thinks of cities wiped out by a single 'bomb'. That in comparison with what was used was nothing. However, the immense pain, the disease and the crying, the tears and death was no different and will never be when the 'physical' experiences *war*. This happened over one million years ago.

That statement is going to sound like utter 'poppycock' (your *mind's* word not ours) when they, the scientists, the researchers say, "Can't have! Never! Impossible! Where is the evidence? Where are the facts?"

We are not going to explain every facet and every detail but say, 'Who do you think made you?' Go and take your mind back to what we said at the very beginning! You, the planets, space, your love and your very essence of life is and has been created by the Great Spirit. The 'Creator' - God. How easy do you think it can be to hide facts and to cover over to let 'humankind' grow once again? You will know the answers when and only when your heart is ready to accept and your 'soul' can *rejoin* in the all knowing. There is nothing that the Creator cannot do. Everything is light and light is you.

This raises a very interesting point because some people will try and twist our words. "Didn't you say the Creator never interfered?" To this we reply:- "We stated that until this 'near' time that lies ahead in your destiny, there will be no intervention, no stopping or raising of a 'hand' to assist or blow you a kiss. All to this point is your *own* doing.

However, because you are light, love and life and will always remain the light, the energy source remains and remained. . . to rebuild again. So you see, because everything is connected and in a circle of light and life, you were reborn from the light's need to be nurtured <u>in</u> light and to be grown <u>with</u> the light - The Creator's energy. Is that easy to grasp at this stage? (PAUSE)

The second time that caused destruction was in the thinking that humankind could channel and misuse the globes' resources in the wrong way. The harnessing of energies which eventually backfired and blew you all away.

We are not talking of something like the progression of 'life' from the seas and through the dinosaur 'eras' that were made extinct from a *collision* between *two* moons! (That will get you thinking. . . the debris and it's impact collapsed and fell upon the Earth). The attempt was to push the boundaries of the Earth's energy 'flows' and mass too far. It was fatal in trying to reshape and divide the world into what was 'owned' by one 'country' and what was owned by another too.

You might think, 'that's such a crazy thing?' Isn't something very similar happening but with a hand on a gun in many parts of the world at present. A *warning* of repetition? This happened about one and a half million years ago and again regrowth and new light replaced and reshaped the darkness that remained.

The third event took your lives away and will, if you follow *this* with your heart, hopefully make you sit up. Perhaps re-awake your life's light to hope and to pray and to rekindle the desire to save you this time. Starting with today?

Almost two million years ago. . . this was the *first* time of your existence as you actually perceive your physical selves. So sad. So, so sad that there was such a fine line to success and to progress yet humankind's 'past' overstepped the mark into trying to expand and evolve far too quickly. The search for the outer knowledge backfiring in a catastrophic way.

'Man' wanted to search the horizons that lay beyond the physical 'Earth plane' and whilst we all say there was nothing wrong with that. . . it was horrific. It was what was taken from *living things* that shook you flat.

A way of utilising energy from many life forms was devised - an extraction of life force, of chemicals, enzymes and energy from many animals that existed then. This was then made into a 'vaccine' for preserving your physical state, a so called 'elixir' of life. The 'Man' of the era wanted to physically live forever and because (as we said earlier, you have all got to similar stages of existence) most were believers. Vast species of mammal and animal alike became extinct.

It was 'man's' quest for everlasting life that destroyed him. The whole balance of civilisation was destroyed and 'he' with it. Only upon death, was everlasting life realised. What waste, what neglect. "What they deserved" many 'beings' have said. But. . . you were reborn and all life again with you. A chance to succeed and to grow in harmony with light and love once again. (PAUSE)

Well, what do you think of what we have said - Gone too far? Are we, and have we, 'gone off our heads'? We have said all along that truth is in the eye of the beholder. To those that can feel the love and light, nothing will seem to be too far fetched. Accept or deny - this truth or just a pack of lies.

Q12. How old can a 'soul' be?

COMMUNICATION: Well, just from what has been read and said, you can now determine that a soul can be at least two million years old. This can be a confusing issue and we would like to clarify it.

A soul can be born at any moment, any moment at all. The Creator sends out it's love and light, as rebirth and birth always and it always has. If we had said that from the very beginning a soul can be born you would say, "When was the beginning?" Here you are deceived again into thinking of 'time' - Humankind's method of course which is important to and part of your existence. Forget 'time' for a moment, for if and when you do acknowledge your very essence it will become easier to comprehend and understand.

When someone puts out or blows out a candle flame, it is true that your 'physical' cannot see the light, so does that mean you cannot see? If you put your hand *over* the flame, does it cease to burn brightly when you move it away again? It remains constant, never to diminish if it is protected from the outside influences that could extinguish it.

So you see, the light is ever growing and everlasting in many forms, always returning after the darkness has come and cloaked your heart. There was and never has been a beginning, there will never be an end. A soul is as old as when the light gave it 'life' and a soul is as new as when the light gives it 'life'.

You reading this could be new or old. It does not matter as long as you *learn*. For example, you could be one thousand or ten thousand years old!

It is not important if you have gone from the darkness and cold to return to the warmth of the Creator.

Q13. Re these communications. At the start of July 1995 when such beautiful information started to flow through, it seemed it was from a different 'source', was this the case? It was as if it was coming from an Ascended 'Indian' Chief. I thought this, as 'White Cloud' was first mentioned. Can you explain or confirm this?

COMMUNICATION: Oh my son, you know by now that we are all one.

There are two parts to this and the first is your 'progress'. As your vibrational level became clearer and higher and reached out through your Soul Star and Stella Gateway Chakras, you then attained a higher level of communication - *not a better one* - it is not and never has been egotistic. Every 'plane' of existence has it's truth(s) and love to tell and to show.

You were indeed progressing in receiving information as you came through and it was beautiful too wasn't it! You learnt of 'Love' and light . . . has the essence now been grasped?

Healing hands were another message and that rings true, to many others including you. Healing energy within everyone of you, but often unbalanced and the channel unprepared. A voice was saying, 'listen, reach out and (to) realise your gifts on the outside and inside your heart and in your mind?'

There are no limits to what can be attained by those who wish to continue their inner journeys once their choices have been made.

You can all be the highest source of communication that you can become. But there is no quick and easy way for most. There must be no resistance and barriers that we mentioned earlier. We hope that you all 'become' and do the best you can, for in that we will know the light that will be created will enable you to achieve your pathways and fulfil your destinies.

ME: Finally, I am sure there are things that you wish to make known to us.

COMMUNICATION: David, for this and our thoughts we just say that in wisdom, knowledge and understanding we do not force anyone to believe what we say. An open heart and mind is all we ask. . and to pray.

Pray with your love for the *love* that you all deserve this time around. The *love* that will sustain and keep us all 'safe' eternally. Everything that you could all ever wish for is with you already. Understand this and you will understand us and for those that need that little extra encouragement - to understand themselves and their 'self'.

Time to relax now my son. Today and yesterday you have done well, not a piece of flattery but to say that soon it will be time to tell. On 'Resistance' (to acknowledge and understand) *you do not have to believe* what we show or say. It is up to you to learn and to pray.

Goodbye from us. Love to you all. Love, peace and truth as always.

ME: Thank you for your lovely words and for your love that you have sent with such peace. Praise be to the Great Spirit our Creator, bless you all.

TUESDAY 28th NOVEMBER 1995 10.40 p.m.

ME: Please enter my thoughts. I wish for love and light to cast out any darkness and sin. Praise be to the Great White Spirit. It is funny how I feel so weird. That this is not an end as such, but a finalisation, an 'episode' of life. . . and my life.

Yet. . . and yet rebirth, a new start too. A new beginning to be embarked upon to show and to tell, one that I look forward to with my open heart.

COMMUNICATION: Bless you David my son. It is funny (we think) how you have lit two candles today. The remains of one previously alight but to then extinguish two. How apt, how poignant yet you didn't know this did you? You could see that as one light fades, a new one is brighter now to lighten and 'enlighten' new areas and new people's hearts and minds.

You look up at the first candle again which is still glowing David. Why does it still continue to burn and to shine so? You could relate this to the love that you bring - it tingles and makes our heart's 'sing' and ring.

A light, a flame can be put 'out' in the physical sense but is never, ever in the truth and love that we have described and we hope you have all felt somewhere in the corner of your hearts.

We have spoken and read and delved into your mind and heart many times David since the connection was made and our communication began. We do not wish to flatter you or boost any 'ego' that you have or to make others seem that you are above yourself. We just want to say that we are proud, very proud of you for the 'time' we have spent together and the openness that you have displayed and the searching that has enabled us to be with you.

You have offered no 'resistance' - no barriers to us and to what our task is to achieve and to accomplish. Let us say that you have helped us, as much as we have helped you my son. We can always learn 'anew' just as you *all* can.

Closed minds equals closed hearts and vice versa. You have been open and honest and also sent thoughts back to us and questioned us too. *No-one* can say we have ever run roughshod over you. All along you have been an individual, but also a symbol of a gathering of light. Sometimes when you think you have been all alone and sitting with the pen aflow, many, many have joined and sat round listening and concentrating on what has been said and what we and you know. Much light and peace together with tears and happiness at your acceptance have poured out from hearts for you and for all humankind.

We are not saying here that this work and this book is for everyone or for even a 'million'. For those and 'that thought' will be decided by the actions and feelings of those who are now searching out from their shells and pushing away the invisible walls that surround them. The way they live and the way that they want to live and become.

Everything is down to the individual as we have said before, but it will depend on the *linking* together that really counts. The 'light' produced, will it be enough?. . . We know that if people open and accept new ways of thinking and being and not just to accept every written word as fact in this book (that *would* surprise us) then destiny will be fulfilled.

You pause my son and think. . . 'What shall we say next? What will we write? What will be in the text? We are going to end (but no end of course) today. . . yes today my son, is the last part. (PAUSE)

Do not feel sad. . . ever, because our work has only just begun and will be even more fun. There is going to be a gap in our communication though to allow you to complete, arrange, organise, draw the pictures, to produce and collate, present and to fulfill this work.

Occasionally from time to time you will feel it necessary to join us and we know this as we are here for you always. These odd occasions you will know in your heart because it will come from deep within you. Our love and your love is never to be broken. No pressure or resistance can break it. (PAUSE)

Remember when we said that it does not matter when and where you are or how you are feeling, and that love is the Divine force in the whole Universe? Once anyone has felt 'love' you would never want to forget it's truth and feeling. We hope that others who read this book can understand what you may be feeling as even a fraction of it will do.

Oh my son. . . dry your tears. . . we love you so. Your tears say more than any words and they are worth (as are anyone's) more than all the riches in the world or Universe. True love and true light is forever sharing both day and by night. It is never extinguished but is often diversed and misguided. We wish to say our final words in a poem from us to you all. To be what you can all be. To be both true to the light and to thee - yourselves.

'RESISTANCE'

We have come with an open hand,
a hand of friendship and a hand of light.
Words and pages come in many forms upon many hands,
but all need to lead to the same goal and to glow so bright.

These communications we have been able to send,
are and can only be judged by yourselves, to manipulate or bend.
Any truth is, and can only be received by an open heart,
it does not come half-hearted, for misuse or a pretence.

There are many many 'beings' and sources of help to you all,
if you look and try to turn within you can hear the call.
Drop those false directions and inclinations that you need to question,
find your light, your glowing flame and your own true direction.

We have not come to say to you all or point a finger,
and what we have described may seem sometimes to disagree with what you know.
This is called 'progress' or a tail with a right 'stinger',
or a calling from way out there (but inside you) willing you all to grow.

We hope and pray that you turn from darkness and decay,
a gentle growth and flow and turning to the light... is the way.
We hope you talk and discuss what this is all about,
to trust in your abilities, your gifts and do not cry or shout.

The barrier, the final wall is yourself and only you,
you stop yourselves being what you can become and also do.
Believe in freedom, truth, peace and democracy for all,
hear and feel the love that is there for humankind, in every living thing and on all 'fours'.
The Divine, The 'Creator' awaits each loving cord,
to return the homecoming 'sun'.
Your new home awaits all those who have light and love in their hearts,
a 'plane' for all to reside, and each becoming one.

Here's a final question, "would you wish to take part or to then ignore?"
By making up your minds, if we have gone 'on' to be a bore.
But if this has changed the way, you live and think,
we know that you will swim . . . eternally, not sink.

Our love for you has always been and will never, ever die,
even though you sometimes stare into the light and cry.
Do not be confused, but seek the answers your heart's why?
For the light will lead you on because your physical's do die.

Goodbye for now my friends, until you hear from us again,
live in peace, harmony and truth. . . loving words are from this pen.
The living flame continues, forever and each day,
climb and step into the light, it is your real. . .

'PATHWAY'

N.B: David, a little note just for you my son. Look to the place where we have mentioned. We will be there for you, watching you, listening to you and your heart. Thanks for what you have done David, . . . we will never, *ever* part. (PAUSE)

Goodbye for *now* . . . always love, truth, in peace and us. . .

ME: The candle faded and 'died', yet of course in real terms it did not. The emotion, the feeling of well-being and peace and also. . . the pain of parting (even though temporarily) was too much. It overwhelmed me and I felt as if 'I', my 'heart' was being torn in two.

Some may feel or seem that this is strange. How, after all I have learned and been through (and with the Transleations, too) do I feel this way? I fortunately (is that the right word?) have never experienced the loss of 'someone' (in this lifetime) that I have been 'close to' but this feels more powerful than anything I have ever gone through. A pain, a ripping or stretching of my very soul. . . yet why, when in this very moment of time, I know that I *will* see and hear them again?

I pass this on to you who read this. If you have faith in yourself and a conviction of love, truth and the light, nothing can or will be impossible.

A PERSONALISED P.S.

After the last 'communication' and completion of Chapter Twelve, I thought, well now it is time to start putting everything together and to start typing the book. However, during a dream on 18th December 1995 I was so excited to know that another 'communication' was to take place.

After this, I experienced the most wonderful meditation and visualisation just a few days later. I could say that these were a 'N.B.' or a 'P.S.' to myself but really I feel they were a message for us *all*. Here then, is what happened.

MONDAY NIGHT 18th DECEMBER 1995

I had gone to bed at 11.40 p.m. and had said a few prayers. I had also been concerned over one of the dreams I had received last night and so I had asked that (tonight), my dream guides would protect me and would come to guide and help me. . .

I awoke at 6.20 a.m. - (just before the alarm, thanks Spirit) from two dreams and it was the second in particular that was to make me sit up and think 'wow!'. In this second dream I sat in a classroom at school and a teacher was conducting a lesson.*

(Here then are my original notes and this is the main part of the second dream).

During this 'lesson' I dropped my pen and picked it back up. After a few seconds, someone else dropped their pen next to me and I picked it up for them too. I looked up to see a beautiful girl.

Her hair was so light and fair and she had lovely light blue eyes. (I recalled this because she put her finger to her eye and touched her eyelid/eyelash.) We then left the building and I walked down a road with her. She then went through a doorway to another building.

I glanced behind me. . . suddenly someone, another girl came around the corner and I immediately knew it was this girl's SISTER. "She went that way" I said. The second girl (same fair hair, etc.,) then replied, "She had left something behind!" "Oh, right" I said. I then had fadeout** and I suddenly woke up.

---

*Researching ones 'records'. Hall of wisdom/learning. Teacher - inner guide, and "teacher".
**Where my vision, image just fades/'blurs' over in my mind.

Like a thunderbolt blast in my mind, my first thought a split second later. . .
TWO SISTERS! I couldn't believe it! The Transleations. . . !

Clairaudiently I then received 'yes' vibrations over and over again. It was like I *knew* that they wanted to communicate again to me. I started to piece together the dream in my mind.

a) Classroom and teacher (GUIDES AND TO LEARN SOMETHING)

b) Pick up a pen (FOR AUTOMATIC WRITING)

c) Pick up the pen again (TO HELP SOMEONE ELSE)

d) Two girls - Identical (THE TWO SISTERS!)

e) Something left behind (A MESSAGE?)

Strange and funny this, because only the other day I wondered what they, (the Transleations) were thinking of the book and I really hoped they would speak/communicate soon. I then thought to myself. . . 'Tomorrow night I am going to see if they will come through. . . '

TUESDAY 19th DECEMBER 1995 6.30 p.m.

ME: The Great White Spirit - the Creator, my teachers, my guides and the Transleations. . . after the dreams and their meanings last night/this a.m., I feel and *know* that this is one of the times that re-communication, re-connection to the higher frequency is to take place.

Bless you all and I love you all so much. To know that you are here guiding me, loving me, teaching me and protecting me is more than I could have ever, ever hoped, yet. . . I know you also want me to move 'forward' and onwards in the correct way. My destiny.

Please let this pen flow at this time for I know there is something important you wish to tell me or want me to know. P.S. I will always love you and miss you so. . . (PAUSE)

COMMUNICATION: David, David, oh my son. We hear you, we hear you and we see you calling our name. In the dream you received last night (yes) it was us and the message you deciphered well, for us to connect and for us to tell. Bless you my son. . . dry your tears with love from our hearts.

188

We feel, as you just felt. . . the rush of energy - an expansion upon the connection. Yes, beautiful too. We have missed you as much as we know you have missed us, but as you write these words your heart lifts. It was as if 'we' or you have never been away. My son, we haven't. . . and never will. We love you and we always will.

If you could imagine many faces and many friends holding their hands around your candle light right now. . . David you are a small flicker of the 'flame' that is growing each and every day, but do not despair at all the bad things that are around you. It is always so easy for us to say, 'do not cry at others pain or misfortune' but you can do no more than shed and guide your light and love to others and to complete your tasks that you and us and the Great Spirit has set for us to achieve. You are as you all are - very special indeed.

You feel warm now don't you, when at first you felt cold as you sat 'still'? You will always be warm when you draw close to us. Always. We have placed a 'shield' around you to keep you in 'place' - not restrained or under lock and key, but one of safety with an inner awareness of the freedom that awaits you all of the truth and love and the light. (PAUSE)

Oh it is so good to let this flow to you and we are so pleased that you can let yourself be able to link as you have done in the past. You have wondered more recently of linking with the frequency and this did not go unheard, even though it was only a fleeting thought in your mind.

Your prayers are answered even though (as many do) you sometimes think they are not. Everything is connected and answered/fulfilled in simple yet also complex ways in the order of events. No-one can by-pass or interfere with the chain or fate of anything that is correct and meant to be. Yes, things can be delayed. . . but what comes around, comes around. Always the circle, always the circle and the web of life. So, even when a prayer is said and an individual may feel and think nothing has ever happened - it will have and *will*, because it *would be* and *would* 'meant' to be.

When we last spoke through you, we did say that there would be times that we would need to get back in touch, that is why the dream came to you last night so that you knew. 'AH!' you say, a purpose or another to your dreams and from your dream guides and teachers in more ways than one. You are getting better at the interpretation and this will improve further because, for you, there *will* be a job to do.

You have listened to your 'within' and persisted and carried on where others have stopped (but not failed). There is no failure in progress or an individual's 'development' ever. Someone can only gain. Whether this becomes a standstill for no more advancement of their heart or if this is their 'following' and their desire it is always up to themselves. NO outside influences, which can seem illusionary or deceiving to others. Ultimately, it comes down to the individual (and their choices).

So *you* knew this morning we were drawing close with the feeling that this brought and you know that the happiness was here with the peace and truth and the love too. We feel it too, especially at your realisation of it. Fantastic could be a word you may use.

David, we are so pleased at the progress you are making, but never fall into the trap of self-righteousness or become, as we have said before, something you are not. We know you will be okay, but we would say, (others may disagree) - play it safe and think carefully from the heart and the mind when faced with choices you are not sure of and then conclude to *your decision* and no one else's.

In regard to 'our' book then this is especially more so. When you have prepared it totally (which you will do and it will not take as long as you think) go where *you* think and feel it will be best received to be mass produced. When that day comes you will get a little extra help in the form of another 'helping hand of light'. Someone will actually show or say something which will help sway your 'mind's choice' to be the right one. You will know because you will *feel* it!

Before this day, you have already been shown a door to speed things along. Take it, for the heart is pure and you can help each other along. You know who I mean and we do not and would not normally say any other person's name on the earth 'plane' but yours, but this is going to be an exception. Speak to *Sheila** again and lift each other's hearts. She has a gift that needs an extra 'nudge' - she will learn and grow with it. Our love goes to her and you all, remember this always.

We wanted to say we liked your pictures and they will fit in well with what is written. Continue them. We know that you are concerned that these won't come out 'right' but they will, don't worry. Someone either at the source of publishing, or publication will fine tune them or perhaps an outside interest will lend a hand.

---

* Sheila, a very dear friend and work colleague.

You must never feel that everything or every single speck of/or detail rests on your head or hand. Just remember you are proceeding with your heart and not with every ability going. Does the tailor of a suit make it too? Does the supermarket grow it's own food? Does the doctor prescribe from his own home-grown medicine? In nearly every walk of life we rely on someone or another.

We keep reiterating that you are all never alone, even when you are lost, cold or starve of hunger or thirst. They are all conditions that envelop your very being, your individual 'pathway' and destiny. Turn within and find that you are one. You are whole, always and forever. (PAUSE)

David, we will need to leave you soon but this short time together has been so lovely. We know you can sense the energy patterns and energy flows that trickle and rush around and within you. . .

ME: Suddenly two beautiful 'images' came to me. The first - like a gathering of forces and hands - closing in around a brilliant flame, a light. Such peace and love. Then the second . . . I could see Millanderer's face and light flowing forward. A feather 'pen' and beautiful pink flower coming from the light, which in turn supported the earth. The earth, a globe surrounded by streaks of golden light which contained words and messages of hope and peace and love in all directions. Amazing.

COMMUNICATION: The love and light that you 'saw' and felt at the beginning and just a moment ago please draw and paint them from your heart and add them to these few pages. This is intermittent communication my son, but this will form part of what is next to follow in the future. When we first 'joined' and participated together we said there will be the beginning, but no end and so shall it be.

ME: (N.B: I have drawn these pictures. Picture Nineteen: 'THE GATHERING OF LIGHT AND LOVE'S FLAME' page 192 and Picture Twenty One: 'GLOBAL LOVE FROM A PEN OF LIGHT AND PEACE' page 193. Although I have tried to draw them, perhaps you could try to picture them yourself in your heart and mind.)

COMMUNICATION: This information today, please choose where to place it. . . In 'Pathway' or. . . ? Yes the book was finished in a sense, but there may or may not be a P.S. Always this part will be up to you, but know that it should be used in the collation of things. (PAUSE)

191

PICTURE TWENTY: 'THE GATHERING OF LIGHT AND LOVE'S FLAME'

PICTURE TWENTY ONE: 'GLOBAL LOVE FROM A PEN OF LIGHT AND PEACE'

Bless you my son and for now. . . we say Goodbye, got to 'fly'. (Thought that would raise a smile.) Be happy David, for your life has only just started to flourish in a true sense, over 'where' it will lead to. . . and over each hurdle and each fence. Be brave, be strong and in your convictions flow and let yourself grow.

You will know David, just as you did *today* when this connection is to be made again. Do your best and you will pass your own tests and succeed and thrive on this new 'feed'. Forever in our hearts.

Bless you, *all* those who have drawn close. Goodbye to you all. Love, peace, truth and from me and us and always trust. X

ME: To say that this has made my day. . . well that is an understatement!

My love is to you and for you all. The energy and warmth was beautiful and you fill my heart. You have said so many wonderful things to me and it feels like you have been a 'transformer' - boosting me with the essence of life - a positive charge running through to my core, the love, the light from the Great Spirit of which I will always want more. It is inside 'me' and I am these things that the Great Spirit has created, as we *all* are. It is just so amazing that I can find no words. . . I just wish to say, forever and always, I am you and you are me.

Thank you to all my guides, friends, family and teachers and all who are 'close' tonight. Take my love and light with you and warm your hands too, for I will always be here for you. Forever *one* together!

I would now like to share with you the final 'link' and part of 'Pathway'. This comes from a short meditation (25 mins) at 7.15 p.m. on SATURDAY 23rd DECEMBER 1995 (N.B: Perhaps you could again follow this with your heart and maybe 'visualise' as you read. . .)

I am a light and move up and up through the house and into 'Space' into a tunnel of light. Inside this tunnel of beautiful light I move forwards and upwards and climb steps up high, higher still, until I get to a level where I have to stop.

To the right is the book 'Pathway' in colours of golden yellow and white light. I pick it up and come back down many, many steps and stop above the planet Earth. I stand alone. . . and I tear out page after page and throw them above the earth. Suddenly, each one turns into a beautiful white dove. A dove of peace and they fly around the globe.

I continue down the stairs and I am in an old cobbled street. I am calling out loud with the 'light' that emanates from me. The light, the knowledge and love and wisdom of 'PATHWAY' then flows through the letterboxes of the many houses in a line up a hill.

I continue to move upwards and I know others are following now holding onto the light and *their* pathway. There is a brilliant bright light and I stop. A door opens and overwhelming peace and love pours out. Everyone comes to the door and they each hand me a book of love and light 'PATHWAY', before they enter the light. The peace and love I cannot describe. . . they have returned home. My duty, my service, my job, my love, my guidance - helping others to learn and to live in the light . . . so beautiful the light.

I feel myself returning, but. . . I am still in the light. . . I am back to the place where the Transleations had first given me the 'Golden Key'. The still water, the greenery, the trees and around me, so much peace. I then throw the key back into the water with a feeling I have opened <u>my</u> door. . . so here is the key returned for someone else now. This is an opening for someone new so that they can grow in some way too, as I do not need to hold onto something that is now part of me forever and cannot be erased. . . and now I am back.

Oh Great Spirit, our Creator, all of my family, friends, teachers and guides, thankyou from my heart for everything. This was, and is *all so very special*. . .
THE 'PATHWAY' TO LOVE AND LIGHT AROUND THE WORLD.

If the Earth
were only a few feet in
diameter, floating a few feet above
a field somewhere, people would come
from everywhere to marvel at it. People would
walk around it, marvelling at its big pools of water,
its little pools and the water flowing between the pools.
People would marvel at the bumps on it, and the holes
in it, and they would marvel at the very thin layer of gas
surrounding it and the water suspended in the gas. The
people would marvel at the all the creatures walking around the
surface of the ball, and at the creatures in the water. The
people would declare it precious because it was the only
one, and they would protect it so that it would not be hurt,
The ball would be the greatest wonder known, and people
would come to behold it, to be healed, to gain knowledge,
to know beauty and to wonder how it could be.
People would love it, and defend it with their lives,
because they would somehow know that their
lives, their own roundness, could be
nothing without it. If the Earth
were only a few feet
in diameter.